PRAISE FOR HYPER SALES GROWTH

"Jack Daly stands above all others. His energy is matched only by his genius and understanding about what makes the best sales organizations. It's not commission strategies, it's not about glossy sales materials; it is about people. Jack understands better than most that if you look out for your people and insist that they look out for your customers, the result is unprecedented growth (and a lot of very happy and inspired employees and customers)."

Simon Sinek, optimist and author of *Leaders Eat Last* and *Start With Why*

"Winning teams result from strong cultures and leadership driven systems and processes. In the world of sales, as detailed in Hyper Sales Growth, *Jack Daly knows how to lead and win."*

Pat Williams,CO-Founder, Orlando Magic, author of *Vince Lombardi on Leadership*

"If you want to play the piano, you hire a teacher. If you want to run a fast marathon, you hire a coach. Jack Daly is the best Professional Sales Coach in America. He teaches you what you need to know, how to remember it, and how to practice it every single day. This book will change your life as a leader and a salesperson, and you will thank Jack Daly every day you make a new sale."

Willy Walker, Chairman and CEO, Walker & Dunlop

"It's finally here! The book all the million fans (that's literal) of Jack Daly have been wanting – a book that shares the same time-tested sales management techniques that work to drive the growth he's been teaching in his powerful and packed workshops. It's all about getting the sales management piece right – and this is the book that shows you the way."

Verne Harnish, author of *Mastering the Rockefeller Habits* and *The Greatest Business Decisions of All Time*

"If you want to get predictable revenue and profitable growth, Jack Daly is your source for the state of the art in sales. Read this book, buy it for your team, follow his advice and you'll be unstoppable."

Christine Comaford, executive coach and presidential advisor; New York Times bestselling author of *SmartTribes: How Teams Become Brilliant Together*

"Jack Daly is the master sales trainer and this book gives away all of his secrets. A must-read for the professional salesperson."

Jaynie Smith, Author of *Creating Competitive Advantage* and *Relevant Selling*, consultant and speaker

"Jack Daly is a rare gem in the business world. I have seen him transform several companies, by growing revenue, by upgrading corporate cultures, and by growing employees' capacity to produce results. His vast knowledge and experience gives him a perspective unmatched by anyone I've experienced. This book is a must-read if you are interested in taking your company to the next level in the most direct way possible."

Rick Sapio, CEO, Mutual Capital Alliance, Inc.

"The most powerful thing a business leader can do is to get people to WANT to do what needs to be done. Jack Daly is that kind of leader. When he writes a book, I read it! You should too. He'll show you how to create the culture, the mindsets and the skills that will separate your company and your team from the pack. Jack lives his message and you can see it in his life as well as his business. Get some of that energy for your business today."

Jim Cathcart, author of *Relationship Selling*; Sales & Marketing Hall of Fame inductee, 2012

"No one person's mentorship and teachings have had a bigger ongoing impact on the sales growth of 1-800-GOT-JUNK? than Jack Daly."

Brian Scudamore, Founder & CEO, 1-800-GOT-JUNK?

"Jack Daly's greatest strength is simple genius: He knows that to grow a business, you must first grow people. I love that he believes in people. It's why I believe in his philosophy. There's a reason he's been at the top of his game for this long."

Brad Meltzer, #1 bestselling thriller writer, host of History's "Decoded" and award-winning comic book author

"For the last 25 years, I've had the chance to learn from some of the best "culture builders" in the world of sports. If I had to pick someone in the world of sales to learn from, it would be Jack Daly. Passion, experience, knowledge–he brings it all in this book. You'll be better if all you read is the introduction!"

Don Yaeger, Eight-time *New York Times* bestselling author; former associate editor, *Sports Illustrated;* speaker

"*Hyper Sales Growth will become a bible for those sales professionals who aspire to 'push beyond their personal limitations' and reap the financial and family rewards that follow! Jack Daly is one individual whom I both respect and trust in the art of Sales Leadership."*

Kathy Cummings, Executive general manager third party and mobile banking, Commonwealth Bank of Australia

"I have known Jack Daly since 1994 and I know him extremely well. He was my business partner for several years as we built the 10th fastest-growing company in the U.S., the #1 fastest-growing company in Los Angeles and won Ernst & Young's Entrepreneur of the Year. This book is a must-read for anyone who wants get their sales force to perform at the highest level, for anyone who wants to build an energizing culture and anyone who wants to get the most out of life. On this topic, there's no resource in the world better than Jack Daly."

Mark Moses, speaker, coach

HYPER SALES
GROWTH

HYPER SALES
GROWTH

*jack*DALY

Street-Proven Systems & Processes. How to Grow Quickly & Profitably.

Advantage®

Published by Advantage, Charleston, South Carolina.
Member of Advantage Media Group.

ADVANTAGE is a registered trademark and the Advantage colophon is a trademark of Advantage Media Group, Inc.

Printed in the United States of America.

ISBN: 978-1-59932-438-8
LCCN: 2014932555

This publication is designed to provide accurate and authoritative information in regard to the subject matter covered. It is sold with the understanding that the publisher is not engaged in rendering legal, accounting, or other professional services. If legal advice or other expert assistance is required, the services of a competent professional person should be sought.

TreeNeutral

Advantage Media Group is proud to be a part of the Tree Neutral® program. Tree Neutral offsets the number of trees consumed in the production and printing of this book by taking proactive steps such as planting trees in direct proportion to the number of trees used to print books. To learn more about Tree Neutral, please visit www.treeneutral.com. To learn more about Advantage's commitment to being a responsible steward of the environment, please visit www.advantagefamily.com/green

Advantage Media Group is a publisher of business, self-improvement, and professional development books and online learning. We help entrepreneurs, business leaders, and professionals share their Stories, Passion, and Knowledge to help others Learn & Grow. Do you have a manuscript or book idea that you would like us to consider for publishing? Please visit advantagefamily.com or call 1.866.775.1696.

"The master of the art of living makes little distinction between his work and his play, his labor and his leisure, his mind and his body, his education and his recreation, his love and his religion. He simply pursues his vision of excellence in whatever he does, leaving others to decide whether he is working or playing. To him, he is always doing both."

—Lao Tzu

TABLE OF CONTENTS

· ·

Part One

Workplaces That Work: The Importance of Company Culture

Part Two

Thinking Like a Coach: The Essentials of Sales Management

Part Three

Birth of a Salesman: Learning to Sell to Anybody

Conclusion: Ironman Lessons Learned

ABOUT THE AUTHOR

Jack Daly is an experienced and inspirational sales trainer and sales coaching expert, offering dramatic keynote and general session presentations, in-depth seminars, and lively sales training courses that inspire audiences to take action in the areas of sales planning, customer loyalty, and personal sales training. Jack draws upon 20-plus years of business experience, including several stints as CEO of fast-growing companies. Jack's previous role as a sales trainer has helped him craft "street tested" sales trainer methodologies. His professional sales trainer know-how has turned him into an accomplished sales coaching authority and author of books including *Real World Sales Strategies That Work* and *Daily Sales Motivators*.

Jack specializes in public speaking, webcasts, e-training, and sales training courses. His history as a CEO and entrepreneur has provided him with first-hand knowledge of the sales industry and how to make the most of any company. His sales coaching workshops, such as "Smart Selling," tackle street-tested techniques that reinforce accountability, territory planning methods and identification of new priorities. Jack's "Sales Summit" course covers sales coaching and goal-setting parameters for accounts and ongoing personal development.

Jack's "Smart Selling" sales training workshops rejuvenate audiences, giving them a newfound understanding of their own skills and capabilities in the workplace, including how to build a world-class sales organization, sell through value, develop a winning culture and retain great salespeople. Sales coaching knowledge combined with hands-on sales training courses are just two reasons why you should know Jack!

A PERSONAL NOTE

. . . .

When I turned 60, I decided to take a daily photograph of something going on in my life. I put together a photo book called *A Year in the Life of Jack Daly When He Turned 60*. It changes your game when, every morning, you find yourself wondering, "What am I going to do today that will make an interesting photo?" I am pleased to say that I have done plenty, and I have plenty left that I wish to do.

I ran my first marathon when I was 46. I did several more in the years to follow, but I really picked up the pace after 2004, when I saw these words on the shirt of a fellow racer as he passed me: "I ran a marathon in all 50 states." I decided to go for it. I now have 35 states completed, and I'm knocking out about four to five more a year. I'm also running a marathon on all the continents. Only Antarctica remains, but it's on the list!

I was 57 when I decided my time had come to train for the Ironman competition. I waited years before taking it on because it requires so much training. I was building companies and raising my family and didn't want to shirk my responsibilities.

The Ironman starts with a 2.4-mile swim, and I didn't know how to swim. I spent a year getting one-on-one coaching and training and practicing for the swim. Then I bought a bicycle and practiced for the bike portion, which is 112 miles. At least I already was a runner, and I certainly needed that stamina: The competition finishes with a 26.2 mile marathon.

A year later I did my first Ironman, and now, at age 64, I've done 13 full Ironman competitions and 30 half Ironman competitions. I'm doing an Ironman on all the continents; the only one I have

jd

left is Asia, which I'll do next year. I qualified to race in the world championship for Ironman in Hawaii, which is the ultimate goal. I gleefully crossed the Kona finish line in 2013. In 2012 I represented Team USA in the world championship long course triathlon championship in Spain.

I'm also playing the top 100 golf courses in the United States. I've completed 82. I'm an extreme sports guy too. I bungeed at the world's first bungee site, Kawarau Bridge in New Zealand, and at the world's highest at the time, Nevis Highwire Bungy, also in New Zealand — within two hours of one another. I dived with great white sharks off the coast of South Africa. I hang-glided in Rio de Janeiro.

Meanwhile, in my career, I average 200,000 air miles and 125 speeches a year. It's a busy life. It's a good life.

Throughout my life, I have put my goals down in writing, enlisting people to help me achieve them. I make a quarterly report to what I call the board of directors of my life: five people who hold me accountable to my goals. Every year I review my goals and share them in detail. Then, quarterly, I look at what went right and what went wrong, preparing for the annual report.

People tell me that my annual list contains what some people would do in a lifetime. They're astonished at how much I intend to get done before I'm dead. To which I say, "If I have a tombstone, all it will have on it is my name with a check mark."

ACKNOWLEDGMENTS

In 1986, I had the occasion to hear Jim Pratt speak at our top sales performers annual recognition event. Little did I know then how fateful that day would be for the balance of my life. I consider Jim to be more than a friend and life mentor. In many ways he filled the shoes of my Dad, who passed on early in life. From that initial day of listening to Jim share his wisdom with our team, I decided we needed to spread his wisdom throughout our growing company. Over the next six months, we travelled to each of our company's 20-plus offices, catching up with each other along the way. Jim was making such a positive impact on our company, on me as a professional and as a person, and all the while seeing the world with his wife Nan in many fun ways. Eventually I told Jim, "Someday I'm going to do what you do". He shocked me by stating that if and when I was ready, he would drop everything to work together, and we indeed did just that! Thanks Jim for life lessons you've shared that have shaped so much of who I am today. To quote you, as I so often do: "No worthwhile effort is ever lost." I'm paying it forward my friend.

I am a guy who has charted my course in life via a "to do list". For better than a decade, I've had on the annual list to write and publish a book which would represent my proven systems and processes for sales and business success. Never would I have thought that a chance meeting at Yankee Stadium would lead to the book you are holding today. Thank you Adam Witty and the Advantage Media Group team; you filled what had previously been a shortfall in my goals! My book is real, and it is "in my voice." I know the Yankees were playing that night, but I don't have any memory of who they were playing or even who won. As far as I'm concerned, I won. Adam approached me in our box, mentioned he was in my sessions earlier in the day, and explained he and his team would see to it that "my book indeed got published." There are many on the Advantage team that made it happen in such a professional fashion, so I thank you all for making the impossible possible.

Over the past two decades I have had the occasion to share business-building ideas with many CEOs and business owners. Many have become such great friends. Our initial contact came through CEO organizations through which I have been invited to share ideas from the speaker platform, including Vistage, TEC (The Executive Connection), Young Presidents Organization (YPO), Entrepreneurs Organization (EO), and CEO Global. While I have indeed shared with many, many have shared with me, and together they have contributed in many ways to this manuscript. Thanks for the lessons, the opportunities to share, and for the good times and friendships.

As a serial entrepreneur, I have had the occasion to work with many fine professionals. I'm reminded of this question: "Who learns more, the teacher or the student?" Well, as the leader of many of these teams, all I can say is THANKS for the learning — it's shared in this work.

My passion is speaking and sharing what I've learned in my business journey. It sure is fun to be so busy, and to make such contributions. Without my team supporting me as a speaker, I likely would have burnt out by now. However, we agreed that I would essentially do just three things: 1) speak; 2) travel to where I speak; and 3) have fun. Jennifer Geiger, my Business Manager, has been with me for much of this speaking journey, and it's been a pleasure and competitive advantage to have her arms around all else that needs to be done- thanks Jen.

I was 16 and she was 15 on our first date and without my wife Bonnie along the way, life sure would have been different. Imagine in our 44-year marriage to date, having lived in 25 homes! The sacrifices she has made, along with our two children Melissa and Adam (now all grown up), so I could do all I've wanted to do, are the zenith of love and support. I regularly fall short of the mark in conveying my THANKS, but I know writing this book once again demanded their understanding. Well guys, we can check this one off the list! It might be nice if I said, "That's it!" but you all know that just wouldn't be true! You guys are the best, and, as George Bailey was fond of saying, "I'm the richest man in town!"

INTRODUCTION:
FOUNDATIONS FOR SUCCESS

I started selling at seven years old. I owned the market for my product and charged twice what other kids asked. That business was making potholders and selling them to moms and grandmoms in the neighborhood.

I had figured out that only little girls were selling them. Eventually their customers would tell them: "Sorry, but I already bought from Mary, Sally, and Susie." If I heard that excuse, I'd reply, "Yeah, but those are all girls. You've never bought a potholder made by a little boy. Would you like one, or two?"

I didn't share the market, as the girls did. I owned it, and when you own a market, you can charge what you want. That was my introduction to the arena of sales.

At the age of 12 I built my first company, in the Philadelphia marketplace. I took over a newspaper route of 32 customers, and a year later, I had 275 customers. I liked the money, but I didn't like the work, and the Philadelphia weather can be crappy. I had to go to school all day, and my parents insisted that I should do my homework and do it well. So I didn't really want to be out delivering 275 papers in the snow, the ice, the cold, and the dark. I wanted to do what I did well, which was selling.

You had to be 12 years old to have a newspaper route, so I hired five 11-year-olds to work for me. "I've already built your route for you," I told them. "Here are the customers. I'll give you half the money the company pays me. I have to buy the papers whether the customer pays me or not, but I'll guarantee you your money. And I'll even take care of the collections." Of course, that last part meant that

I got the customers' tips. I never agreed to share those tips, which are most of what a newsboy makes.

My system meant that my employees did all the work while I kept 70 percent of the money. I was honored as Newspaper Boy of the Year. I called the company and said, "Why hasn't anyone ever asked me how I did what I did?" After they leaned my tactic, they hired me to teach other kids how to sell.

That story underscores the importance of leverage: the generation of more business and money with less work. As a newsboy, I didn't like doing the deliveries. What I really liked, and what I was good at, was generating subscriptions. The company was interested in that too. But as long as I was out delivering papers, I was so busy that I didn't have time to do what I could do best.

Today I find salespeople all over the world who are making that mistake. In effect, they are out delivering newspapers. They're doing things they shouldn't at the expense of generating new business.

FROM CADDY TO ACCOUNTANT AND BEYOND

In school I was formally educated as an accountant, but that path started at the golf course. I became a caddy at a private country club when I was 13. At first I thought my job was to carry clubs, find balls, rake traps and such. But after a couple of weeks, I realized that these golfers all had nice cars, big homes with pools, and a lifestyle far better than my parents had.

I saw this as an opportunity to learn from these successful people— and that's what I did, all summer. I peppered them with questions: "How did you become more successful than most people? What did you do differently? What would you not do again? What would you tell a 13-year-old who wanted to be successful in life?"

You can imagine the conversations among the adults at the clubhouse: "Hey, have you ever had that Daly kid caddy for you? Did he ask you those questions too? You know, I'm going to follow up with that kid and see what he does with all that." I had a country club full of mentors who were taking a vested interest in my success.

I learned that you need to have goals, and a process and a system to ensure that those goals take place. Many entrepreneurs open up businesses but don't understand how to be profitable. "Go and get formally educated," my mentors said, "and learn how the numbers work."

I became an accountant and worked for the Arthur Andersen firm. I had never really aspired to be an accountant, but what I learned in becoming one led to my success as an entrepreneur. The most important two words of that education were "systems" and "processes."

The largest sales force I ever led had 2,600 people. "There aren't 2,600 best ways to sell this stuff," I told them. "We're going to figure out the best way and have a system and a process to manage the business accordingly."

I became a serial entrepreneur, building six companies from a blank sheet of paper into national firms, all of which grew fast in revenues, sales, and profits.

FOUNDATIONS FOR SUCCESS

Many asked me, "How did you get these companies to grow so quickly and so profitably?" That is what launched me into what I've been doing the last 20 years: speaking engagements and corporate training in sales, sales management, and business entrepreneurialism.

The principles that we used in my companies, as well as in my youthful experiences, are the foundation for that training. I focus on what leads to success: the importance of leverage, and of systems and processes. Through leverage, you can generate more business with less work, while systems and processes promote uniformity and consistency.

Sports teams, whether professional, college, or high school, are run better than most businesses. The teams practice. They have game plans. They have systems and processes. And they learn to leverage opportunities to score.

Using those principles, I have built systems and processes to teach companies how to improve their organization and sales, and how to build winning cultures so their people enjoy working for them and perform accordingly.

....

I encourage you to visit www.jackdaly.net for additional resources to improve your business. While there, sign up for my monthly e-mail newsletter.

....

IN THE REARVIEW MIRROR

I've had the opportunity to look back in the rearview mirror of my life and see clearly the importance of three indispensable factors in building a successful company. First, you must know where you want to go. In a word, you need vision. You also need key people in key spots, because you can't do it all yourself. And you need to develop a thriving business culture in which your people look forward to the journey. Let's take a closer look at those elements of success.

Vision

When I talk about vision, I don't necessarily mean creating a mission statement, though that is important. I'm talking about something grander, about the very thing that motivated the entrepreneur in the first place. What was that spark of excitement that led to that leap of risk?

Think of it as the painted picture (thanks, Cameron Herold) of one's dreams, the one worth risking it all to make it happen. If the vision is magnetic and compelling, people become excited about what the company is all about. It's the vision that also gets us through the tough patches that we are bound to run into as we go about this entrepreneurial journey.

Visions look to the future, yet also focus on today so that the workforce gets as excited as the entrepreneur does. The vision should be shared with coworkers so they have no doubt about their role in how the company makes money. With such clarity, businesses thrive.

Key People in Key Spots

I've spent decades building businesses and meet hundreds of people aspiring to grow their businesses. When I ask them what they mean by that, they tell me that they want to grow their revenues. In other words, they want to grow sales.

For most businesses, the way to do so is to grow the sales force in quantity and in quality. When you do, those salespeople in turn will grow your sales. That is why, as you try to get key people in key spots in your organization, you need to carefully consider who is in charge of growing your sales force. That person plays a crucial role in your success. And yet I have often witnessed three sins of sales management that weaken businesses. Let's take a look at each of those sins.

One sin is committed when the CEO or owner wears the hat of the sales manager. If you are doing that, you basically are relegating both the CEO job and the sales manager job to part-time status. In effect, you're saying, "I'm going to grow my business part time." If you want your business to grow, you must grow your sales force, and you need someone doing that full time.

Another common sin of sales management is to take the best salesperson and make him or her the sales manager. It can work, but seldom. Usually you just lose your best salesperson and get a mediocre sales manager. The role and the responsibilities are entirely different. A salesperson's role is to win new customers, nurture the ones you have, and differentiate you from the competitors. A sales manager's role involves recruiting, training, coaching, building, and developing. To be good at one job doesn't mean you will be good at the other. Salespeople are used to immediate gratification, from deal to deal. Sales managers, by contrast, must take their time in recruiting, training, and coaching. A salesperson might easily become disenchanted with the pace of the new role and look for another sales job, perhaps with your competitor.

The third sin of sales management is probably the most grievous of all. The best salesperson is made a sales manager, but he or she is also required to continue booking business. It's absolutely ruinous. Their focus remains fixed on the customer, as that is how their compensation is driven. Accordingly, the sales team is underserved, missing the opportunity for leveraged growth.

Each one of the three sins has the effect of minimizing the sales management role, and effectively holding the company back from achieving its growth. Small to medium businesses tend to go into one of two directions. They stay small to medium, or they go out of business. When you ask why, it most often comes down to a violation of one or more of these three sins of sales management. Having key people in key spots is absolutely the secret to success.

Culture

When I think about culture, I think about how I might encourage an environment in which employees don't wake up each morning and think, "Oh God, I've got to get up and go to work again today." Instead, how about an environment where the workers get up every morning and say, "Hot damn, I get to work at a great place!" They feel that they get to go to work instead of have to go to work.

If we could only get right those three factors for success—the vision, the key people, the culture—then everything else in business would be easier. Unless those three are working in sync, all business endeavors will be more difficult.

This is a book of practical strategies, not theory. This book is based on real-world ideas that work and that are easy to implement. What's in this book has been street tested in over a hundred industries all over the world, and it has proved effective at the personal level and at the company level. These strategies increase top line revenues and sales as well as bottom line profits.

None of this will work if it stays inside this book. You need to take action. Unfortunately, over 70 percent of the people who attend sessions or read books on how to do better in business don't take action. You can have the best ideas, the best strategies, the best tactics, the best systems, the best processes, but none will work unless you take action.

I recommend that when you read something in this book that resonates with you and motivates you, flip to the back where you will see blank pages under the header, "Take action." Take a moment to jot down what you plan to do. After you finish the book, look at all your notes and write down some dates for when you plan to accomplish those action items.

I wrote this book as if you were attending one of my live sessions. I try to write the way I talk. You may notice, for example, that I call people "guys," whether they are male or female. I grew up near Philadelphia in Pennsylvania, and that's the way we talk. In the Rocky movies, when Sylvester Stallone referred to "the guys," he wasn't concerned about their plumbing. Nor am I. I'm just concerned about whether you do a good job at bringing in business.

PART ONE

WORKPLACES THAT WORK: THE IMPORTANCE OF COMPANY CULTURE

CHAPTER 1

. . . .

AN AIR OF DIFFERENCE

*"The two resources your competitors can't copy
are people and culture."*
— Eric Flamholtz

I have often asked business owners to tell me their greatest sales challenge. More often than not, they talk about a lackluster sales force. How, they ask, can they motivate their salespeople to get out there and bring in the additional business needed for their company to truly prosper?

The answer is that you can't really make people become motivated. You have to hire them that way, and then you need to create the culture in your business that releases their own motivation. In this book, I will be telling you much about company culture, sales management, and sales techniques. I will make it clear why this matters and how much it can mean to your bottom line.

Let's start, however, with a look at three companies that I believe are models for creating the kind of culture in which salesmanship thrives. They have grasped the essence of what I will be explaining in this book. Let's pay a visit to Southwest Airlines, Zappos, and the Virgin Group.

SOUTHWEST AIRLINES

Southwest Airlines has taken that lesson to heart. It has been in business for about 40 years and has made money every year. In its first three decades, it was primarily led by Herb Kelleher, who was in the forefront in saying the key to Southwest's success would be its culture. The company has been consistent in its approach.

Gary Kelly, the current CEO, writes about that culture in a company magazine that travelers find at every airline seat. In his article, *The Southwest Culture: Our Secret Sauce*, he writes: "I ask three things of our employees every day: Work hard, have fun, and take care of each other." What the company has said comes down to this: "If we can create an environment in our business where the people who work in it don't get up and begrudgingly come to work but get up and are excited about coming to work, we'll have the competitive edge."

I average about 200,000 air miles a year. I have senior status with a lot of the airlines, but I can say that of all of them, the one whose employees look as if they enjoy what they do, flight after flight, and convey that enjoyment to their passengers is Southwest Airlines. You can even see it in their dress: They wear shorts in summer, golf shirts, and running shoes. Employees of other airlines are dressed as if they're being punished.

Southwest encourages its employees to have fun and interact with customers. I was on a flight where the attendant said, "Hey y'all, pay attention to me up here. I'm about to do the safety announcement. For those of you who haven't been in an automobile since 1954, here's how a seat belt works." Everyone in the plane was laughing.

I related that story to Herb Kelleher, who told me, "Well, it seems not everyone was laughing." He said he got a letter from somebody complaining about that employee. The company should not be making fun of something so important as safety, the letter said, and that unless Kelleher changed the policies and procedures, that person would never fly with Southwest again.

"What did you do?" I asked.

"I sent the customer back a note that said, 'We will miss you.'"

That's a leader making sure that the employees are treated well and that the company stands behind them. In fact, Southwest Airlines once had a billboard campaign on highways throughout America. The billboard made three points. "The customer is not number one. Our employees are. Because if we get it right with our employees, they get it right with you, our customers."

That is the power of culture. If you can create an environment where the workers actually enjoy what they're doing, they'll convey that enjoyment to the customer, and magical things will happen. That's the power that Southwest has tapped into.

Delta Airlines and United Airlines, which have been losing billions over many years, operate gates right next to Southwest Airlines. They tried to copy the Southwest model. United gave birth to an airline called Ted, and Delta gave birth to an airline called Song. They thought that the magic with the Southwest Airlines formula came from not assigning seats and things of that nature. What they didn't address was the culture. They just replicated the old culture of United and Delta and put them into the Ted and Song Airlines, neither of which succeeded.

I have traveled many miles with American Airlines and very often I'm a carry-on-luggage guy. One day I arrived a few hours early in Chicago for a flight home to Orange County, California. I looked at the departure listing and noticed an earlier flight to Orange County, leaving in 10 minutes, so I ran down to the gate in hopes that I could get on.

At the gate, I asked the attendant if I could make that flight.

"Sir, that's not what I do," she told me. "You need to go back to the ticket counter."

"I just want to know if there's a seat," I told her. "Maybe I could get on."

"You're not listening, sir. I'm busy here. You need to go back to ticketing."

"I'm just hoping you could find out for me while there's still time," I told her. "After all, I have superstatus with American Airlines, with millions of miles ..."

She didn't let me finish. "If you continue to do this," she said, "I will have security remove you from the airport."

So I went over to the Southwest Airlines gate, where a flight was soon to leave for Orange County. "Hey, is there any chance I can get on this flight?" I asked the gate attendant. "I've got a later flight two hours from now on your airline." The attendant asked if I'd checked my bag and then peered at the computer and said, "Yeah, go ahead. We've already boarded, but take any seat that's open."

It's an entirely different way of operating your business. One way is trusting and empowering your people. The other way is to have so many rules and regulations that the customer no longer cares to do business with you. I happen to think that it's probably more enjoyable to be a Southwest Airlines employee with the liberty to have some fun and a little levity, to put smiles on customers' faces, to feel you have more than "just a job."

Southwest Airlines communicated the importance of getting planes up quicker than anyone else. By working together and eliminating "it's not my job" from employees' vocabulary, Southwest opened more gates in more cities and offered promotions and raises and job opportunities. Everyone won.

In spreading the word to employees on how the company makes money and the employees' role in it, Southwest is eloquently simple: "Wheels up." In other words, if it can get its wheels up more quickly than the competitors can, it will be in a more secure position with more opportunities for people. The company has created a culture where its people act in the best interest of both the customer and the company. It's more than just a job.

All of that is being led at the senior management level under this blanket called culture. One might think that Southwest, a public company, would trade on the market as SWA. Instead, it trades as LUV. Love. Love the employee and love the customer, and everything else will take care of itself.

ZAPPOS

At conferences and speeches I ask my audiences, "How many of the companies represented here today are more than 10 years old?" About 90 percent of those in the room raise a hand. I say, "Well, this is going to be like giving blood. After the sting is over, you're going to feel really good about your donation."

Two years ago, Zappos, in its tenth year of existence, sold the company to Amazon for $1.2 billion. Amazon basically bought

Zappos for one word: culture. You can witness that culture in a one-hour tour of the company's headquarters in Las Vegas. About 900 people are employed there in what Tony Hsieh, the founder, calls the sales and service area. Zappos doesn't distinguish between sales and service.

The people who work at Zappos would rather be there than at home or out with friends. A lot of companies preach about values and their mission statement. But I've been on those Zappos tours, and I have gone off-tour to ask employees at their desks about the values of the company. They were quite articulate. Each year, Zappos publishes The Culture Book, which people are given at the end of a tour. Hsieh asks employees to send him e-mails saying what it's like to work at Zappos. They're unedited. In essence, the e-mails say this: "This is the best. I'll never leave here."

Zappos does some things very differently than a lot of other companies do. Like Southwest Airlines, it empowers its people. It is in the business, primarily, of selling shoes online. If you were to call for a specific pair of shoes that you couldn't find online with Zappos, the employee would help you find those shoes somewhere else and make a note that the company should start carrying that line. Zappos has a culture that encourages employees to spend time on the phone with customers—and I can tell you from experience how important that can be.

I was hired by a company based in New York that had an inbound sales area. The company wanted me to increase its sales. I listened to the calls being received. The salespeople weren't spending enough time asking questions and learning the real needs of the customer and building rapport. They seemed to be trying to get on and off the phone quickly. I taught them to slow down, ask questions, develop rapport.

Within three months, the company experienced a doubling in sales. I was asked by the senior management to come up and meet with them. I thought that I was going to get a pat on the back, and what I got was a kick in the butt. The kick in the butt came because the "abandonment rate" went up. The abandonment rate is the measure of how many people get tired of listening to bad music as they wait on hold and hang up. That's an abandoned call.

What happened was that as salespeople spent more time with their customers, more callers got tired of waiting. I looked at the managers and said, "Well, listen. If you had hired me to improve the abandonment rate, I could get that to zero and I could do that in a week, but you hired me to increase sales, and I did that." One of the guys turned to me and said, "Well, go down and reduce the abandonment rate then." I said, "Wait a minute, let me make sure that you want me to do that, because I'm going to go down and I'm going to tell them that every time someone calls they should just say hi and bye. We won't have any sales, but your abandonment rate will be zero."

The answer to curing the abandonment rate was not to hurry the call. The answer was to either slow your marketing down and reduce the number of calls, or put more people in the seats to answer the calls. Don't accept bad sales behavior.

Zappos understands the importance of spending time with customers. The more, the better. In fact, they actually know and track who the record holder is for the longest call with a single customer. This is a company that sells shoes online, one pair at a time. The longest call in a single transaction was eight and a half hours.

I'm not suggesting that people spend that much time on the phone, but when I talked to the company about it, here's what the staff said. What they're looking for isn't the sale. Salespeople are taught that their goal is to find a way to make the customer feel loved. A happy customer comes back and refers others. In the first eight years when Zappos was in business, it didn't spend a dime on marketing. All of its business was repeat and referral.

At Zappos, people look forward to going to work and being with friends. They're empowered, recognized. They feel their voice counts. They can dress casually. Tony Hsieh sits in a workstation out on the floor with the other employees. The company has a nap room and a playroom, and the cafeteria is open all day and night, at no charge. The people want to work there, and as a result, the customers rave about what it's like to do business with Zappos. As a result, after 10 years, the company ends up being purchased for $1.2 billion.

Anyone hired for any position at Zappos goes through a three-week paid training program in sales and service that instills the company culture. Zappos offers a check for $2,000 to leave the company if you don't think you're a good fit for that culture. Three people a year, on average, take the $2,000. Everybody else turns the money back, in effect saying, "You couldn't write a check big enough for me to turn this job down. I want to work here more than anywhere else."

That's what makes business boom. Customers feel the difference and tell others. You attract better people and keep them longer.

Most businesses aren't operating that way. It's hard to understand why they don't when you consider the power of leverage: more money with less work. One way to take advantage of leverage is to figure out how others make money doing it. That what I was doing when I interviewed members of my country club that summer when I was 13. And that's what Zappos clearly understands.

VIRGIN GROUP

Many businesses find themselves mired in the muck, but if you hire the right people and establish the right culture, they will make sure you don't get into that muck. That's what Richard Branson has done with his phenomenally successful Virgin Group.

A couple years back, *Playboy* magazine interviewed Branson. "Is there an overall lesson on how to keep a company vital?" he was asked. To me, that question meant, "How do I create a winning culture?"

This was the essence of Branson's response: "It all comes down to people. Nothing else comes close. Motivating people, bringing in the best. You assume every switchboard operator will excel and they will. Often, people make mistakes, but you allow for that too. Praise people. Like plants, they must be nurtured. Make it fun."

It's fun at Zappos. It's fun at Southwest Airlines. And here is Branson, saying, "Make it fun." There is a common denominator among these companies: They are places where people want to be. They are fun.

"Keep it vibrant," Branson said. "Everything comes back to people, nothing else. You get loyalty, enthusiasm, and great service for your customers."

Here's a guy who, in our lifetime, built an empire of more than 300 companies. He is not caught up in the "muck" of daily issues and operations. He's not doing what so many other business leaders are doing: he isn't pulled into so much of the day to day. To me, Branson comes across as the company cheerleader. I recently saw him on television wearing a blond wig on an airplane; he had lost some sort of bet with an employee and was playing the role of a flight attendant. Wherever he's out in the public eye, he seems to be having a lot of fun.

When I talk about that, some business leaders tell me: "If I had the kind of money that Richard Branson has, I'd be out having that kind of fun too." But Branson was doing that when he didn't have any money. He didn't start with money. He started in the record business and went out of business, but he's resilient enough and creative enough to thrive. He has long had a loyal following because of the culture he has created of empowerment, fun, recognition, and reward. He draws people to him.

"YOU CAN'T FAKE THESE THINGS"

"You have to start with culture, values, and a commitment to creating a fantastic workplace," says venture capitalist Fred Wilson. "You can't fake these things. They have to come from the top. They are not bullshit. They are everything."

Venture capitalists invest in emerging companies that they think will be successful so that they can cash out at a big multiple down the road. They are looking for quality. And it speaks volumes that Wilson says the kind of companies that a smart venture capitalist will want to put money into are the ones like Southwest Airlines, Zappos, and Virgin.

In the world of sports, one coach who figured it all out was John Wooden. He won the national basketball championship 9 out of 10 seasons. He had figured out how to create the systems and processes and to create the right culture that focused on the basics. He knew that if his team focused on the basics with consistent systems and processes, then the scoreboard and the standings would take care of themselves.

I can remember years ago watching UCLA win championship after championship. Wooden just sat in the bleachers with a rolled-up program and never got emotional. Sometimes people would ask him why he wasn't running up and down the court. He said, "If they haven't figured it out before game time, it's too late then." He focused on process, consistency, and practice.

Most business owners don't take that approach. They are fixated on the financials, comparing actual to planned. Where did this variance come from? They're micromanaging the numbers. They would do better to focus on the systems and processes rather than the scoreboard. That's how they will get the results that will beat their competitors.

That is what Branson, Hsieh, and Kelleher are doing. They are focusing on the systems and processes to build a winning culture. That way they don't have to micromanage their people. They have such a differentiated level of service that the customers come back time and time again.

If you feel that you have become mired in the muck as you try to run your business, then you may be eager to try something fresh, something that will pull you out of the quicksand and set you free to grow. I offer you these three examples of company culture in the hope that they will inspire you to reach for the possibilities. In their stories, you can see what it takes to succeed.

CHAPTER 2

· ·

WHAT'S IN IT FOR YOU?

"The office image and work commitment created in the first month,
first day and first hour is difficult to change."
— Jim Pratt

Monday, Tuesday, Wednesday, Thursday, or Friday—which do you believe is the worst day of the workweek to start out a new employee? When I ask my audiences that question, most call out that they believe it surely would be Monday. A few say Friday.

I happen to think Friday is not too bad a day, because it tends to be the least productive day. It affords the opportunity to spend more time with the new hire. I do see the rationale of those who say Monday is the best day. It's the start of a full workweek, after all. On Monday everybody has a list of all the things they want to get done so that they can get the week off to a good, robust start.

Let's say your new hire shows up for work Monday morning and you get a call saying he's in the lobby, waiting for you. You might think, "What the hell! I have a long list of things to do besides show a new employee around." So you send him to HR for a few hours of paperwork, and then you pawn him off on whomever else you can, just so he's out of your hair. Eventually you put a big three-ring binder in his hands and send him to a conference room, maybe with no windows, and tell him to read it.

Was that ever you on your first day on a job? When you were starting that first day, you were probably excited about coming to work—new career, new company, new job. Your significant other probably gave you a hug in the morning and said, "Go have a great day. I can't wait to hear how your first day went." Later, here's how you described it: "It kind of sucked. They stuck me in a room with this book. I hope it gets better from here."

That's how most businesses treat new hires. When I ask business owners which day they usually start new hires, almost everybody says Monday. Maybe it's because that's the start of the pay period. But whatever the reason, it's not the best day. If you don't have enough time to make the new hire feel special, find the day when you can do that. The corporate impression and commitment to excellence created in the first month, first day, and first hour is difficult to change.

Compare that experience to that of a person who has been working in your company for a half a dozen years. He is well loved, a hard worker, but he decides to relocate. He stays three weeks to help you with the transition. Many companies throw a going-away party for such employees. They take them to lunch, as a group, or they take them out for drinks, or they give them a present.

HOW ABOUT A WELCOME PARTY?

I say this: I don't know how there can be a return on investment from throwing parties for people leaving, but I do like the concept of throwing parties for people coming. If you want to create a winning culture, how about throwing parties for new hires?

Imagine entering the lobby on your first day and seeing a big whiteboard that says, "Welcome"—and it has your name on it. "We're thrilled that you've joined us," the sign says.

You walk over to the person in the lobby. In most companies that person is called the receptionist. In our company, that's the Director of First Impressions. That's what it says on his or her business card. That's what it says on the tent card on the desk where that person is greeting the new hire in the lobby. Where do we start getting a sense of a company's culture? Right as we walk in the front door. That Director of First Impressions is critical in a winning culture.

You check in with our Director of First Impressions, who says, "Oh, we've heard so much about you." The director tells you the company is excited to have you. "I'm sure you've heard about our mission and values," the director says, "but did they tell you just how special it is to work here? It's so much fun, doesn't even feel like work. Everyone wants to be here." Could you hire somebody who would talk like that to a new hire? Absolutely yes. The right person in that job would do just that.

And then the Director of First Impressions would turn to the new hire and say, "Hey, let me take you back to where you'll be working." And there you see streamers hanging from the ceiling and circling your desk. Balloons are tied to the back of the chair. There's a card signed by the owners of the company welcoming you aboard. There's a welcome card signed by the team that you will be working with.

There's a company logo shirt on your desk, and a company logo ball cap on your desk. A box of business cards has been prepared for you, a far cry from the approach of some supervisors, who say, "Here are 30 of my cards. Just scratch out my name and write yours." What kind of a welcome is that?

Then we have sandwiches brought in for the entire team, and all of the guys take about five minutes to say how long they've been there and what they're doing and what their family's like. Then you get 15 minutes to tell your story. Then we assign a peer to you for the next 60 days as the go-to guy so that you don't have to go to your manager time and time again and say, "I don't remember how this software works." You go to a peer because it's less threatening.

I'm thinking that at the end of the day, after you put on your new shirt, tuck your new cards in your pocket, and go home, your significant other will ask, "How did it go, honey?" And you will say, "Gosh, you wouldn't believe it. I made the greatest decision I've ever made. I walked in and my name was in lights in the lobby, and they took me to my desk and they had streamers and balloons." Then your significant other says, "Yes, I had a sense that it was going to be like that. Look at this. They sent a bottle of wine home and said we should crack it open over dinner and celebrate the beginning of a great journey together."

That costs me perhaps $100, depending on the quality of the wine. But what a difference it makes for an employee looking forward to coming in on Tuesday, Wednesday, and Thursday. Incidentally, all of your friends and associates knew that you changed companies and changed jobs, and the next time that you saw them, they wanted to know how the new job was going. You likely said, "This is the greatest place I've ever worked. Let me tell you about what my first

WHAT'S IN IT FOR YOU?

day was like." That's when your associates said, "Hey, let me know if they're ever hiring."

It's an incredibly different experience but one done by design. We figure out how to welcome new employees much better than our competitors so the people in our company will go out into the marketplace and talk about what a great, fun place this is.

....

Visit www.jackdaly.net and sign up for my monthly e-mail newsletter for an ongoing supply of such ideas.

....

THE FIVE O'CLOCK STAMPEDE

I recently was delivering a presentation in Toronto at the prestigious Fairmont Hotel. When I was finished, I needed to talk to another group about three blocks away. I headed up the sidewalk, where I was confronted by an onslaught of humanity. People were spilling out of buildings in mass and running. "What the hell is going on?" I wondered. "Is there a bomb scare or something?" I asked about it later and learned that right across the street from the Fairmont is the train station, and I happened to be there at about 10 minutes after five o'clock.

What that told me was that the majority of people were clock watching, disappointed with what they were doing, and couldn't wait to be released from the prison of the day.

When you walk through Zappos, it's an entirely different environment. The people are not clock watching, and they're not unhappy. We see the same thing at Google. You may have seen it in *The Social*

Network, the movie about Facebook. These companies have figured out how to create environments where people enjoy what they're doing and where they do it. They lose track of time.

As a consultant, I'm often with a business owner in his or her office. Let's say it gets to be 10 or 15 minutes after five. I find a reason to look out the window at the parking lot, and I see people stampeding to their cars. It's as if the business owner and I are the only two guys who didn't get the notice that there is a bomb in the building. There is no reason that would happen if you create an environment where people enjoy what they do and get lost in their work.

A FUN WAY TO GROW

I arrived in California in 1985 to build a company, and we grew it in 18 months from four people to 750 people. In our first three years, we made $42 million in profits. I went on to another company later in my life, and in 1993, two partners and I built a company that, five years later, was recognized by *Inc.* magazine as the tenth, fastest-growing, privately held company in the United States, with 10,100 percent growth. Ernst and Young honored us as Entrepreneur of the Year.

If you were to interview me or my two younger partners in that company and ask us what differentiated us, we would tell you, hands down, it was our culture. It was the sense of fun. Any of the employees who worked for us would say, "I've never worked anywhere else that was as much fun."

Those fun companies were growing exponentially on the revenue and the profit side compared to our competitors. We had an easier time of recruiting. We had a lower rate of turnover. People wanted to stay because the leadership designed a culture that would be rewarding and fun and manifest itself in good business practices, with systems and processes.

And at five o'clock, we didn't have a stampede out the door.

WHAT MY MOTHER LEARNED

About two years after I moved from the East Coast to California in 1985, my mother came out for a visit. By then my company had grown into our corporate location, which was 40,000 square feet on two floors of a high-rise. Proud son gives his mother a walkthrough. It was about six thirty in the evening, and people still were working. I introduced her to them as we made the rounds.

Back at my office, I said, "Hey, Mom, I need 10 minutes to gather my things and then we'll get dinner. Have a seat." She said she'd prefer to take a stroll on her own.

The next morning, Charlene, who ran operations, came into my office. "I think your mom is just a cut up. She is really fun," she said. "She came back and she sat down with me and said, 'Charlene, do you mind if I ask you a couple questions? Are you married? Do you have kids?' I said yes to both, and she asked, 'So why are you still here after six thirty?' I told her I had some things to do and this was a productive time for me. Then she asked this: 'Be honest. Is my son making you be here?' I laughed. 'Listen,' I said, 'your son, most of the time, is out of the office, running around the country. I'm not even sure Jack knows when I'm here and when I'm not here. He just happened to be walking by and introduced you to me. Jack has nothing to do with me being here right now.'"

My mother had come up in a business culture where you only worked a certain number of hours in a certain period of time. Your work wasn't something you wanted to do. It was something that you had to do. It wasn't about choice. Her cultural orientation, when it came to running a business, was that you couldn't have it be fun. In her mind, you couldn't have a culture where people would actually stay of their own volition, such as at Virgin, Zappos, Southwest Airlines, and other companies that are knocking the ball out of the park.

PRESCRIPTIONS FOR CULTURE SUCCESS

Corporate cultures are as diverse as the companies themselves, but when you think about the strategies that I am advocating here, they come down to three prescriptions for success. Let me summarize what I've been saying

First, you must create an environment where people want to go to work versus have to go to work. Some business leaders seem determined to do the opposite. I meet such types on the golf course. One of my life goals is to play the top hundred golf courses in America. I've completed 82. I'm typically traveling and alone, and golf courses won't let a single out, so I have to wait until a twosome or a threesome show up. I don't know these people, so I'm on my best behavior. If someone hits the ball into the woods, I typically hear something like this: "Well, a bad day on the golf course is better than any day in the office, huh?"

This person often is a business leader or owner, and I want to rip the guy's head off. If you, as a leader, feel that way, what, then, is it like, culturally, for the employees at that company? That guy walks around with a mentality that says I have to do this as opposed to I want to do this. And so the first crucial element to creating a successful culture is to create an environment where everybody in the business wants to come in, versus has to come in.

My second prescription is this: Strive to win over the hearts of your employees. If you can do so, your company will have a competitive advantage. The employees will do things voluntarily that you could never mandate. They will come to work early, they will stay late, and they will work on weekends. You will get so much more out of your people if you devote the time and effort to win over their hearts.

My third prescription for a successful corporate culture is to put the F word back in business. Make it fun. Is it fun to work at your company? If you can create a fun environment, we have proof that it will turn into top-line and bottom-line bonuses.

SO WHAT'S IN IT FOR YOU?

Dr. John Kotter, Harvard professor and prolific *New York Times* best-selling business author over a 10-year period, studied companies that spent time managing their cultures well and compared them with companies that did not. He found four key takeaways regarding revenue growth, stock prices, net income, and job growth.

Revenues increased 682 percent in the companies that spent time working on their culture versus 166 percent. In effect, that shows that if you spend time developing a culture, your revenue growth tends to be more than three times what it otherwise would be. As a sales trainer, I can tell you that any company would hire someone who would give it that threefold increase in sales. The Kotter study establishes that focusing on company culture is the key. That is another example of leverage. If you really want to grow your business, here's the way: invest the time, systems, and processes to create a winning culture.

In culture-rich companies, Kotter also found that stock prices increased 901 percent in that decade, compared to just 74 percent for the culture-deficient companies. Stock prices underscore the value of a company, and that's more than a tenfold increase.

In measuring net income—and now we're talking about profits—the results were immense. Net income increased 756 percent in the culture-rich companies over the 10-year period, versus 1 percent for other companies. That means going from barely paying the bills to a profitability growth of 756 percent.

Job growth, meanwhile, increased 282 percent, versus 36 percent. It's not hard to see that company culture works magic. It's the leverage that generates more business with less work—and you will notice that I keep coming back to that concept. You get that leverage when the people in your company are excited about going to work. That's what will give you the advantage over the competition. It's true that culture is hard to define. Your business plan is what you are, but culture is who you are.

FROM BLOCKBUSTER TO NETFLIX

Netflix came onto the video scene considerably later than Blockbuster. Blockbuster had been in the business of renting of videos decades before Netflix was founded. Today, Blockbuster has gone bust. Netflix is trading at an all-time high. Its founder would underscore the importance of company culture as a way to stand out in the market.

Netflix has carefully defined culture policies and procedures, and what it has accomplished is astounding. For example, it used to have an extensive binder regulating vacations: how long you had to work to qualify for how much time off, and when you had to take your days, and many other rules. It was all in the binder. Then, at a company meeting, an employee said, "The vacation policy is confusing. I come in early and I work late for no extra pay, because I love working here. Nobody tracks that time, yet the vacation policy here is to track everything. I don't understand that."

The CEO said he hadn't thought about it that way. After all, he took vacations when he wanted, without reporting to anybody. Therefore, the policy wasn't a big deal to him. It was a big deal to everybody else. When he heard that, he decided to change the policy. Now the binder is gone. The vacation policy at Netflix says simply, "When you need a vacation, take it."

I've told that story to audiences for about two years, and some company CEOs have told me they implemented that policy. They say some people actually forget to take vacations; they are so into their work that they're not even using their time off. Most business owners are hesitant to make a policy change like that, because they think people would abuse it, but if the culture is right, apparently something quite different happens.

Netflix also changed its policy on reimbursing expenses. It used to have a very detailed list of what was allowed and what wasn't, with forms to fill out. Today it's one sheet. It just says, "If it's an appropriate company expense, please bill it to us." It relies on trust and integrity. And as a result, employees feel valued and don't abuse that trust.

In *The Social Network*, you can see, as the scenes unfold, how Facebook is gaining momentum and expanding its staff. In one scene, an employee rides a skateboard down the hallway. As I sat in the theater, I wondered how many business owners would watch that and understand that they shouldn't try to protect a company from that kind of behavior but instead encourage it. You should try to make your company cool. You need to be attractive.

CELEBRATING THE MILLENNIALS

I often hear business owners say, "How do we get these millennials to want to work"? I say it isn't that they're lazy. They'll stay up all night playing video games, and for the right incentive, they'll stay up all night working for you. Google has employees who gave up renting apartments because they were hardly using them and, basically, they live at the company, eating, sleeping, and playing there. It's their whole world.

Take a look at companies that are creating environments where millennials give it all they've got and then some. At Zappos, millennials make up almost the entire staff. I'm not saying every company culture should look and feel like Zappos. But I certainly urge you to take a new look at how your culture affects business.

I recently took a dozen business owners on the Zappos tour. Two of them told me they'd prefer to stay on the bus and skip the tour. They had e-mails to answer and such. I later asked them if that was really why they hadn't joined us. "Well, from what we saw in the lobby, this just isn't right for our company," one of them said, and the other nodded.

What they had seen in the lobby were three Zappos employees who had enough metal attached to them to set off airport alarms. Where there wasn't metal, they had tattoos. They looked like something from a carnival. But their CEO, Tony Hsieh, says he frankly doesn't care how people dress or whether they have piercings and tattoos. After all, the company's business is all online or over the phone.

Still, many business owners want no part of the carnival, and I'm not trying to sell the carnival, nor am I saying you should convert your hallway into a skateboard park. What I'm selling is a broader concept. I want you to see how you can create a unique workplace that doesn't offend or discourage customers or clients but does make employees want to stick around and give you everything they've got. Hsieh saw an opportunity to attract dedicated people willing to devote themselves to a place that didn't prejudge them.

You have to be sensitive to the employees and their expectations and their needs. So much

> *"If you can differentiate a dead chicken, you can differentiate anything."*

has been written about the changing expectations from the Greatest Generation to the Baby Boomers to the Gen Xers to the Millennials, and how each generation looks differently at the workplace. We need to make the environment compatible with the lifestyle that the employee expects or needs.

Again, it's how can you differentiate yourself? How can you gain that precious leverage? Always be on the lookout for creative opportunities. As Frank Perdue said, "If you can differentiate a dead chicken, you can differentiate anything."

YES, A FREE LUNCH

Let me show it to you this way. I have some clients who provide lunches for free to their employees. One of my clients started out with less than 10 people. Each day a different employee would bring lunch in for everybody. The company grew to several hundred people but didn't want to lose that concept of the free lunch. Today it has engaged a caterer, and the employees don't have to pay for it.

Many businesspeople would cringe at the thought of that expense. The leadership of that company laughs to hear that: "They just don't get it. The cost of that meal is so insignificant compared to the appreciation we get from the employee. They're telling us they've never worked anywhere where they were given a free hot lunch every day. And usually, after they fill up their plate, they return to their desk and eat while they continue working."

The guys running the company say that, for $5 or $10 a day per person, they get at least an extra hour of productivity from each employee. The employees win, the company wins, and the customers win. Everybody is happy with the deal.

I have an accounting background, but I can say this with confidence: There are no such things as expenses in business, only investments. What we should be doing is trying to figure out what is the return on investment in that activity. The return on investment for the free lunch program is tremendous when you pencil it out. It's like the return you get from the balloons and wine for employees on their first day.

Many businesses refuse to spend that much. I encountered that attitude from a businessman in Australia, where I speak every year. I spoke about culture and sales to an organization of entrepreneurs. The next year, the organizer asked me back but suggested that I skip the culture part. "Businesses have been hurting in Australia," he explained, "and employees aren't leaving when they know they're lucky to have a job. So frankly, we don't need to focus on culture and creating a great environment."

That guy never got it. He never grasped the concept. The success of Zappos took place during a tough economy. That's not the time to cut back on culture. It's what gives you momentum, but if you look through a prism and see only added expenses, you will sell yourself short. "Why should I do that?" business owners say. "They're lucky to have a job anyway." I hear that attitude a lot.

PARKING WITH THE CROWD

Here's a personal example: I once was hired by a very large company to run its entire mortgage operation nationwide. It was the tenth largest mortgage lender in the United States and wanted to be number one.

I came into the office at 5 a.m. and noticed the parking lot spaces were all marked reserved. Even though I was the number-one guy there, I figured nothing should be reserved for me. I'd never had a reserved spot. I parked around back and waited in my office for people to arrive so I could introduce myself. Out the window, I could see the spots filling up between 8:30 and 9:15 a.m. or so. The technical starting time was 8 a.m. I later learned all those reserved spots were for the leadership and management. The rest of the workforce took the long walk. Some had already arrived when I got there at five, and many arrived well before eight.

I was quick to make my point: "Guys, we're not having a class system here. Nobody has a reserved spot. Those spots go to the first person arriving in the morning. If they're gone when you get here an hour or more late, that's called 'tough-get-here-earlier.' In our culture, we're not going to differentiate in parking."

That's the kind of culture that Hsieh exhibits at Zappos as he sits at a workstation out on the floor with everyone else. When you do that, the people around you respect you for it. You can't get up in front of people in your company and say one thing and do another. You can't tell people how important they are to your company, that they're the most important ingredient in its success and then arrive late and claim the most convenient parking spot. I insisted on that change, and the work force bonded with me quickly. The Herb Kellehers and the Richard Bransons of the business world would have done the same thing. They know that when employees like and respect the management, they'll give their all.

That's the return on investment that I've been talking about. That's what's in it for you.

CHAPTER 3
· ·
LET'S TAKE IT FROM THE TOP

*"If you don't treat your own people well, they
won't treat other people well."*
—Herb Kelleher

I'm a big sports enthusiast. I enjoy participating in individual competitions such as Ironman triathlons and marathons, but I also like to watch spectator sports.

Whether it's the Super Bowl or World Series or Stanley Cup or whatever championship, when the winning team celebrates in the locker room, the players often say the same thing to the reporters: "What made the difference for us is we're a family. We care about each other. It doesn't feel like anything is out of the ordinary to go out of our way. We don't have an attitude like 'I'm a guard and I don't play a forward position.' We help out wherever we can for the benefit of the whole."

That is the kind of attitude that companies need to develop. You want people who don't stay in their silos but instead look for the greater good of the organization and the customer. That's when the magic happens. You win the equivalent of the world championship at whatever sport you're playing or whatever business.

You would never find a sports team sending players in without a game plan. You would never find them putting players out there who haven't practiced. And every good team spends a significant amount of time recruiting. When the players follow the systems and processes, the results manifest themselves in more wins than losses.

My thoughts turn again to Coach John Wooden and the run that he had with UCLA. Nine out of 10 years, UCLA basketball won the national championship. I went to school in 1969 at La Salle in Philly, and we were 29 and 1. We were ranked second in the country. That was like being ranked first, because first was always taken by John Wooden.

On the first day of practice every year, Wooden told his players to take off their socks and shoes so he could instruct them in how to properly put on their socks and tie their shoes. He never wanted to see a player unable to do his best because he didn't put his socks on right and had blisters. He never wanted to have a turnover in a game because someone tripped over an untied shoelace.

Wooden focused on the basics. His teams practiced the fundamentals, and that way he knew the standings and scorecard would take care of themselves. He once saw a UCLA guard throw a behind-the-back pass to a teammate who finger-rolled it into a layup for two points. Immediately, Wooden called a time-out and benched the guard. It didn't matter that the pass was successful. It violated Wooden's systems and processes. He would practice what he preached.

Fast forward from then to now. This past year, in January, the University of Alabama team won the national championship of college football. That's three national championships in the last four years! Here's what was reported about Coach Nick Saban in *Fortune* magazine, September 2012, before the championship game. "What really separates Saban from the rest of the crowd is his organizational modus operandi. In Tuscaloosa, they call it the Process … He has a plan for everything. He has a detailed program for his players to follow, and he's highly regimented. Above all, Saban keeps his players and coaches focused on execution—yes, another word for process—rather than the results." In other words, he micromanages, but with a purpose.

My newsletter readers had this heads-up six weeks before the game. Sign up at www.jackdaly.net.

There is another example of a sports team coach who is turning out terrific results by focusing on the basics and having the systems and processes in place to do that.

Now, this year, just a few months ago, Rick Pitino, the coach of Louisville, won the national championship of basketball. He's the first coach to have won the national championship with two different universities. Within five minutes of the end of the game, the announcers said that the consistency that Rick Pitino brings to the party year after year is the result of micromanaging his players and coaching so that they follow a system and process of consistent application of the basics.

A BUSINESS LEADER NEEDS A GAME PLAN

Whether we're talking about sales, or sales management, or culture, companies need to design their game plans and build the systems and processes to execute in the sales, sales management, and culture area.

Most of the time, the business leaders run the company with financial statements. They compare the plan against the actual. They look at the variance column. They get all wigged out about those variances. That's like a John Wooden, Rick Pitino, or Nick Saban looking only at the win-loss column and score.

In the college football championship this year, it was a landslide victory. Notre Dame looked like an amateur team next to the University of Alabama. The game was over by halftime. What was interesting to me was, in the last seven minutes of the game, the Alabama quarterback got into a fight with the center on his team. They were slapping each other around out on the field because of a missed call. These guys were leading by four touchdowns, and there were seven minutes left. They're best friends, and they're roommates at the University of Alabama. And yet they got into a nationally televised fistfight because of a breakdown in the process that they had practiced all season. If you, as a business leader, could get your people to be married to the process and system of success and practice those things and put them into place, the results for your company would be manifest. Visit www.leveragesalesmgmt.com for the winning sales management systems and processes.

STEPS TO BUILDING A WINNING CULTURE

You must have leadership from the top and get the systems and processes in place before you're going to get anything right. And many companies still just don't get it right. Most companies fail in this all important culture area. There are many reasons. But chief among them is this: People and companies tend to underperform because they rush to the urgent at the expense of the important.

There are four key components to building a strong winning culture. Those four components are recognition systems, communications systems, empowerment processes, and personal and professional development processes. Those are the four legs to a strong culture, and we'll be taking a closer look at each in the next chapter and the next section, but you could have a business and never address any one of those items. Your business won't run well, but none of those four areas are urgent.

When you look at the specifics from Kotter's 10-year study, they are massively important. If we, as leaders, made culture a high priority, the people in our companies would willingly come in early, stay late, work weekends. They would lose sight of time. They would see their work as far more than a job.

A LESSON FROM THE MARINES

I live in Southern California, in San Clemente, adjacent to the Camp Pendleton Marine base. I befriended the general who runs Camp Pendleton, and we went to dinner one night. I was an army captain. Over dinner, the general told me, "Jack, we really appreciate the fact that you were in the service. I know you were in the army, but you'd have to agree that of all the branches of the service, the marines are the best." We laughed, but he said, "No, really, we're the best, and I'd like to tell you why. Let's just do a little exercise. I'm going to give you a word, and I want you to put a visual in your mind. When I say 'navy,' put a visual in your mind. Now I'm going to say 'air force.' Put a visual in your mind. Now I'm going to say 'army.' Now I'm going to say 'marines.' Now tell me. When I said 'navy,' what was in your mind?"

I said, "A ship, a boat."

"All right. When I said 'army,' what went into your mind?"

I said, "A tank."

"How about when I said 'air force'?

"A plane."

"When I said 'marine,' what came to mind?" he asked.

"The only thing I could come up with," I told him, "was a human being."

"Bingo," he said. "That's exactly right."

He said, "Do you know that our training program is double the length of all the other services? Congress is always beating up the marines and saying all the other branches get the job done in half the time. But we will not change our training program because we're trying to change this human being from just a marine into part of the marine family. If he's in a foxhole with another marine, we want him to fight like he's fighting with a family member. Semper Fi.

"Guys who were discharged from the marines 20 or 30 years ago," he continued, "can bond with one another simply by walking up and saying 'Semper Fi.' They understand culture, they understand family, and they understand the work it takes to change someone. It's a great lesson that comes from the top. And that's why we're the best."

THE FAULTY FOCUS IN SALES

Since my focus is primarily on sales and sales management, let's take a look at what happens in most companies in that realm. The training program for salespeople when they join a company is, typically, a three-part training program. It goes like this: Here are your cards, here's your territory, and good luck, baby. Go for it.

We throw them out to the wolves. We don't train them well. We don't have them practicing. We might do some product training, but we don't leverage off a game plan. We don't have a script.

When most companies hire salespeople, they are eager to get them out calling on customers and bringing in business, the sooner the better, and the more the better. Both of those assumptions are wrong.

First of all, it's not true that the more people we call on, the better it will be. What we have found is the top producers call on fewer people yet write more business. The key is they call on the right people. Too many salespeople call on too many people who don't deserve a call.

In most companies, the Pareto principle exists, and that's the 80-20 rule. That's 80 percent of the business is coming from 20 percent of the customers. In most businesses, 80 percent of the business is being generated by 20 percent of the salespeople. The other people are just flooding the marketplace. They're inept because they haven't been trained, they haven't practiced, and they haven't taken the time. Companies are in such a hurry that they just throw them out into the field. As a result, they're killing prospects all over the place. Occasionally, they stumble into a transaction or a deal. They bring it back. Half of the information that they got is incorrect, and it stalls the operation side.

There's this urgency among management and leadership: "Hey, if we get more people in here and get them out into the field, the quicker the better. All our problems will be solved. We will just be engulfed in sales and profits." Then they find out that that's not the case.

Four to six months later, this is what I hear: "Well, we're not doing a very good job of hiring people because we hired this guy five months ago, and he's just not producing." Well, he's not producing because you've got him practicing on real customers instead of practicing inside. You're not even teaching him the systems and the processes that bring success to your best salespeople.

MODELING THE TOP PRODUCERS

Let me give you an illustration. I get hired about 10 percent of the year to speak at the annual awards and recognition events for larger companies. They take their top sales performers off to luxurious resorts, Cabo San Lucas, Mexico, or Hawaii, or the Caribbean. I'm hired to speak for about three hours to the group, but they're there for five days and invite me to stick around for the five days. I play golf, and fish, and swim.

It's a great gig, but I find it frustrating to see the same people going to the event year after year. If there are 100 people in the organization, and 15 to 20 of them are winning the President's Club and are getting to go on these trips, 12 to 15 of the people are the same ones every year. That tells me the leadership is doing a poor job. All the salespeople have the same product and price and service to offer, so if the same ones win the trip every year, they must be doing something different. The leadership should try to figure out what that is, turn it into a system and process, and create a checklist of what they need to do to succeed. See Appendix IV for a template of checklists for sales leaders and sales producers.

That's what Nick Saban is doing at the University of Alabama. That's what Rick Pitino is doing in Louisville, and what John Wooden did at UCLA: modeling the behavior of the top producers. That's what every business leader should be doing too, but, instead, they feel the urgency to just get more people out there in hopes of raking in deals.

If you get the culture right, everything else you do in your business will be easier. If you don't get it right, everything is going to be harder. You have to stay true to your values and your purpose.

CHAPTER 4

. . . .

CULTURE BY DESIGN, NOT DEFAULT

"There is no job that can't be delegated —
except recognizing your people."
— Jack Daly

One of my favorite contributors to *Inc.* magazine is Norm Brodsky. He wrote an article titled, "The One Thing You Can't Delegate: Defining and Enforcing Your Company's Culture May Be Your Most Important Job." This is his opening paragraph:

Building a business is a creative act. Few of us realize when we start out that we are creating not only a company but a culture. That's because it's usually not planned. It just happens. While everyone is focused on something else, making sales, providing service, sending out invoices, a little community springs up. It has its own unspoken customs, traditions, modes of dress and speech, and rules of behavior. By the time you become aware of it, the culture is often well established and it will probably be a reflection of your personality.

Most companies are so focused on dotting the i's and crossing of the t's on their products and services that they forget about winning over the hearts of their people. They overlook the soft side of the house, the cultural side of the house. They are so tied up with the functional aspects that they miss what matters most in motivating a change in behavior.

It need not be that way if they would just pay attention to this critical contributor to corporate success. A business can actually design a plan with activities, systems, and processes, and monitor them for consistency so that the culture becomes a winning one. That way, they would be creating a culture by design, rather than accepting whatever happens by default.

THE NEED FOR CONSISTENCY

Companies that operate in multiple locations face an additional challenge. The corporate office might articulate the company culture one way, but it still could vary significantly from location to location.

Consider, for example, McDonald's restaurants. Let's say I stop at a McDonald's for lunch. The service is swift, with no lines, and your burger and fries are hot and fresh. The place is clean and tidy, and the staff is friendly and attentive. Four hours later, I pull off the freeway for dinner at another McDonald's. The place is dirty, service is slow, the food is cold, the staff is surly. That's the same company, but I will venture to say that the cultures are different at those locations.

The lesson is this: The managers of a business can articulate and design a culture, but they need systems and processes to ensure that it is upheld. They need to inspect what they expect, from one location to the next. The management must be clear about what the culture will be and insist on consistency.

POWER OF RECOGNITION

As one of the four legs of a strong culture, recognition is among those essentials that must be articulated. There is no job that can't be delegated, except recognizing your people.

One simple form of recognition is to send out birthday cards and cards celebrating each worker's anniversary with the company. That increases loyalty and encourages a strong work ethic. It contributes to the esprit de corps. Your competition's employees see what you do and want to work for you. I know that happens, because I've been doing it my whole life. I've had people standing in line to come to work for me.

The CEO of a bank in San Francisco told me he calls every employee on his or her birthday—that's 350 people—and talks for 5 or 10 minutes. "Every night before I leave the bank, our HR person gives me the list of anybody who is having a birthday the next day and their phone number." It's just two or three calls a day at most. He says the employees feel appreciated and spread the word. That guy understands that it's worth half an hour a day to build a better relationship with the people who work in his company. He gets it. But he is the exception. That doesn't happen often.

Notice that he has a system for it. He has his HR person give him the names and phone numbers. He doesn't just say it would be a good idea; he makes sure it happens. At one time, my largest sales force was 2,600 people. I wanted everyone to get a birthday and company anniversary card, so I set up a process: The HR department sent me a packet of addressed cards on the fifteenth of every month so I could add a personal note. "Hey, John, I noticed that you're celebrating eight years with the company, and it's amazing how much progress we have made in that time through the efforts of people like you. Thank you for everything you do for us. We look forward to many years of working together." I signed all the cards for that month and gave them back to HR to distribute when the day approached. People all over the company told me that was the kind of recognition that made them want to work early mornings and late nights and weekends.

It was a process. I didn't have to think about it. There wasn't anything hard about it. We made it easy by setting up a system.

HANDWRITTEN NOTES

There is power in a handwritten note. Recognition doesn't need to be expensive. It just needs to be consistent. A notepad costs little but can be one of the most powerful tools in building a culture. A handwritten note from a leader can become someone's treasured document. People keep them, sometimes for a lifetime. I have a file at my home of every handwritten note that any leader, manager, or owner to whom I reported ever gave me. That file is thin, not because I wasn't a good performer but because company leaders rarely write such notes.

I made it a point to send a note to each of my top 50 salespeople each month. "Hey, Bob, here you are once again in the top 50 of our 2,600 sales people. Six of the last seven months you've been in the top 50. That tells me your customers appreciate you and we do too. The next time I'm out in your area, let's go out and have a beer or two together. Thanks for everything you do. Jack." Later, when I went out in the field, I often would see my notes hanging in workstations.

I walked into my Buffalo, New York, office and saw a collection of my notes in a glass frame in a hallway called the Hall of Fame. I walked into my Colorado Springs office, and a new hire introduced himself. "Look in my eyes," he said as he shook my hand. "My name is Bill Smith. I'm a new sales guy, and I want you to know that before the end of the year, you'll be sending one of those notes to Bill Smith."

I went back to my hotel room at about nine thirty that night. The amount of e-mails and voicemails that I had to address in an organization of 2,600 people was enormous, but I put my phone down and sat down to write 10 handwritten notes before I dealt with any of those e-mails or voicemails.

If I had attended to the e-mails and voicemails first, I might not have gotten to the handwritten notes until midnight, and by then I might have been thinking about my early flight the next morning and decided I was too tired and would write them some other time. When does some other time come? Never. What's the difference between the e-mails and the voicemails and the handwritten notes? The handwritten notes are important. The e-mails and voicemails are urgent. My competitors were addressing the urgent, while I was addressing the important. That is the magic.

A business owner came up to me in Chicago after I had given a presentation. He said, "I want to tell you something about those handwritten notes. I never really thought I'd be running this company, but my dad passed away a couple decades ago and I've been running the company since. This past year, one of our employees passed away. I went to the funeral, and they had a reception at the guy's house. And there I saw, in frames hanging in a hallway, two handwritten notes that my dad wrote two decades ago to this employee."

That underscores the importance of recognition, and handwritten notes in particular. If that's what people are valuing, why not build a system and a process that lets people know that we appreciate them? Don't leave it to chance. Don't wait until you happen to be in a good mood. Don't wait until you think you will have a few minutes. Instead, set up a consistent process and system to implement this easy, no-cost tool: the handwritten note.

OTHER RECOGNITION SYSTEMS

Let me run through several other effective methods of recognition, other than birthday and anniversary cards and handwritten notes.

Planned Spontaneous Recognition

Another is what we call PSR, or planned spontaneous recognition—in other words, a surprise event.

In one of my companies, we had the biggest sales production month in our history. Everyone worked hard. They came in early. They stayed late. They worked weekends. We did everything we could to make the numbers the biggest they had ever been. I was so proud of the whole team that I arranged a surprise. When they arrived for work the first day of the following month, they found seven flip-chart tripods in the lobby. Each had a room number, and it said, "Pick an hour out that you would like your free massage because I've brought masseuses in for the entire day, and I'm giving out free one-hour massages to anyone who would like one as a thank-you for all your efforts last month."

The employees talked to one another for months afterward about those massages and how cool our company was. They talked about it with their family and their friends. This is what they were saying: "I work for one of the most grateful companies in the world. My goodness, have you ever heard of such a thing? I'm telling you, I'll never leave this company. I've never been appreciated more than that."

That wasn't the only way I showed our appreciation. On a hot day later that week, I contracted for a guy in a full white suit to come through the office with a pushcart and bell and hand out free ice cream pops.

People loved it. We're not talking about a big expense. These are little things that make a big difference.

Caught in the Act

Another recognition system that works well is called Caught in the Act. We send a card to people who have delivered exemplary service. The front of the card says, "Caught in the act ..." and inside are the words "... of greatness." The recipients read about what they were caught doing, and learn that they will be entered in the Act of Greatness contest.

Anybody in the company can give this card to anybody else. We went through 30,000 of them in less than 90 days. That's 30,000 moments of people recognizing other people with just a piece of paper. The contest winners, chosen through a drawing, get a DVD player or something simple. But everyone who was "caught" felt good about it. All of this was by design, and it was about winning over their hearts.

"Out of the Box" Awards

Another recognition system is what I call the Out of the Box Awards. A lot of managers talk about encouraging employees to get out of the box: to think creatively, do things differently. Many people resist going outside the box because it's more risky. They're not sure the reward is worth the risk.

When I was 17, I worked in a grocery store, stocking shelves. One day, when I came back from my 15-minute break, I saw a woman in her 80s, hunched over in the produce aisle. She seemed to be having an argument with the vegetables. "How can I help you?" I asked.

She said, "Sonny, I came in for spinach and there is none." She was right. I told her that if she wanted to finish her shopping, I would have the spinach for her in half an hour. She brightened up. In a panic, I drove two miles to a competitor's store and bought six bags of fresh spinach. She was in the checkout line when I returned. "How many bags would you like?" I asked. She said, "Just one." I said, "Here, take two. They're on us. I really appreciate your loyalty to our store." Subscribe to my YouTube channel and receive a regular dose of such gems.

Most employees would have feared they might be fired for that. And if they gave away the spinach, how would they be reimbursed? That was four decades ago. Today, in many companies, employees would never go outside the box that way.

But what if companies rewarded such behavior? Suppose my spinach sprint had brought me a $100 gift certificate, presented in front of the 200 employees of that store? You can be sure that other people would start looking for similar opportunities.

What I have discovered in my business life is that you get the behavior that you recognize and reward. Some companies do this by giving an award for the employee of the month, or of the quarter, or of the year. That alone goes a long way toward communicating to your people that they matter to you.

Ring the Bell

For decades I have had a big marine bell hanging outside my office that all employees can ring whenever they think they deserve recognition. As soon as the bell rings, everybody in the area pauses to see what's going on. Everybody gives the bell ringer a hooray. It's been very effective for many years, and some of my clients have implemented it with great success.

During the Zappos tour, I saw, hanging on the wall, a bell, a whiteboard, and a megaphone. "What's up with the bell?" I asked. The tour guide said, "Well, we have more than a hundred people on the phone out on this floor, and it can be hard to know when they deserve special recognition, so we told them, 'If you ever do anything you think you deserve recognition for, disconnect from the call, come up and write your name on the board, ring the bell, and then shout it out.'"

"Have you done anything worthy of recognition?" she asked me. "Put your name on the board, ring the bell, and tell them all." I shouted something to the group. All of them were talking to customers on the phone, but they all gave me a clap and a hooray. Now, if you were on the phone as a customer with Zappos, hearing this racket and this cheering, I think your reaction would be, "Hey, what's going on over there?" "Oh, we're just recognizing somebody who did something really good." My reaction as a customer would be, "What a great company."

The ring-the-bell recognition is a low-cost, simple, immediate, basic way of helping people to feel recognized and energized. The more we can get people to feel good about what they're doing, the more powerful our culture is.

Digital Photo Cards

As soon as digital photos came into the marketplace, I started running around my company getting pictures of people shaking hands with me for various occasions: a birthday, the completion of a big project, their first sale, the biggest sale, a record-making sale. Whatever it was, I could take a picture of it and celebrate it, and then I would go back to my office and type whatever I wanted on the card. There are online services that will send the card wherever you want. The service that I use today is called SendOutCards.com/jackdaly.

People treasure these cards. They're personalized, they're professional, and they're incredibly effective. Today my iPhone can take the photos. I write the message right on my iPhone. I've got the app for that. It's automatic, and it takes care of it. I'm constantly looking for photo opportunities to send out cards. People love this. I have clients who have implemented that idea as well, with tremendous success.

Contests

This recognition system works well for salespeople in particular. Salespeople love contests. Daily contests, weekly contests, monthly contests, quarterly contests, annual contests—overlapping contests all over the place. The award can be as simple as a $50 Starbucks card. "Whoever rings up the most sales today, I've got a $50 Starbucks card for you. See me at the end of the day for your card."

With this variety of recognition systems, from cards to contests, the effect should be that people wonder each day, "What is Wacko Jacko going to do now?" I want people to look forward to coming in to our company. The challenging question is this: How many of your employees are overly recognized? If I were to ask that question of a roomful of employees and managers who had hired me as a motivational speaker, you can be sure that the managers of most companies would be thinking, "This is not a good start." But the managers and employees of Southwest Airlines, Zappos, Netflix, and Virgin would be confident that they were doing things right.

SEVENTEEN WAYS TO BE A BETTER COMMUNICATOR

Good communication is another important building block for a strong company culture. Let's take a look at 17 keys to communication.

Vision Sharing

Once you understand what the vision of your company is, you need to share it with plenty of people. You should constantly be finding ways to communicate the vision of the company, where you are headed, what you are trying to accomplish. If people see the big picture, the small picture of activities becomes easier to understand. If I don't know where I'm going, I don't know how to get there. Sharing what we're trying to accomplish helps me with my day-to-day functions.

Off-Site Planning

Another key to communication is off-site planning. Some companies call this a "retreat," where the leaders go off for a few days of discussions. I don't agree with calling it a retreat. It sounds as if you should put a white flag up and go backward. I suggest calling it an "advance"—that is, discussions on how to move forward. Whatever you call it, that procedure of going off-site and talking about where your company is going and how you are going to get there is another good tool for communicating within your company.

The Daily Huddle

The daily huddle came out of a book called *Mastering the Rock-efeller Habits* by Verne Harnish. He and I share many clients. Many of our clients have implemented the daily huddle with great effect. When I mention it to my audiences that include many CEOs, about

20 percent report that they do the daily huddle. Many have done a 15-minute huddle every day for at least a few years. They report that it is one of the best things ever implemented in the company. Their people know each day what is happening, what's hot and what's not, and the issues being addressed.

That daily huddle is a tremendously powerful communication vehicle, and I have clients who have 150 to 200 people all getting together at the same time. It's daily and expected. Nobody has to run around the building, rallying people to attend, and it works incredibly well.

Monthly Announcements

With monthly announcements, you just enhance the daily huddle. The understanding is that you are going to cover more material. It's not going to be as rushed, and you will be digging a little deeper.

Quarterly Updates

Quarterly updates are even longer and stronger than monthly announcements, and they get even more in depth into our business. If I have outlying locations, I might record a DVD of those quarterly updates and send it to them so they can listen in.

Quarterly Themes

Some companies decide on a theme each quarter. For example, the theme of the quarter might be "We're going to the moon." The moon is X dollars in sales. They will set up a chart marking the progress to the moon with a moving spaceship. Theme posters will be placed around the company. If you get to the "moon," there are rewards and recognition and celebrations. This is a great communication vehicle to reinforce how you are doing, and everyone sees the chart and posters as they pass down the hallway.

E-mail Blast and Voicemail Blast

These two are similar, working in different communications media. In one of my businesses, every Friday at 3 p.m., I would sit at my desk and do a 20-minute to 30-minute blast to the voicemail of every employee in our company. Thousands of employees received that voicemail blast. I would recognize some top producers. I would announce new products. I would talk about how we performed as a company that week. I would talk to them about challenges in the company and what we were doing about them. I would load it up with all kinds of information.

If you're the leader of the company, and you know everyone in the company is waiting on Friday for that three o'clock voicemail blast, you will have to be actively figuring out all week what is going on in your company. Because you're that involved, you become that much more effective as a leader.

Communication is a two-way street. It's not just talking to people. It's listening to people. When you listen to people and then communicate back to them, by way of these e-mail blasts and voicemail blasts, what you're hearing and what you're doing as a result, this is what your people think: "The leadership team respects me. They care about what I'm thinking, and they do something with what I'm talking about." That motivates them to go above and beyond the call of duty.

Annual State of the Company

This is yet another extension that enlarges the daily huddle, monthly announcements, and quarterly updates. That's where we gather everybody together, we do recognition, we do rewards, we do a synopsis on how we performed as a company last year against our plan, and what our new plans for the next year are. We re-emphasize our vision for the company.

Newsletters

Newsletters are simple. I'm not talking about a newsletter from the typical HR department. I'm looking for a newsletter that the employees look forward to getting. It has stories of success. It has recognition. It has testimonial letters. It has some information about the company's performance. When employees receive it, they stop what they're doing and take a look at it. They go home and share it with their significant other.

Orientation

Orientation is how new employees are treated. As I described earlier, a welcome party brings a far better return on investment than a going-away party. The time to throw a party, with balloons and streamers and cake, is when they arrive, not when they leave. And new employees should never be shuttled around or left in a room to do paperwork on the first day.

Reorientation

I have found that in working with companies that begin to throw parties for people upon their arrival, longtime employees would start grumbling, as if to say, "They treat the new people way better than they treat the people who have been here for years. They never threw a party for me." We have to be very sensitive to this. What I say is: when you're going to introduce something new like parties for new hires, you also need to do something for all the people who are already there.

When I started to hear complaints that we treated the new people better than the long-timers, I had pizzas brought in for all the employees of all locations and said, "I wasn't here when you started, so let's just call this even. I'm going to throw a pizza party and pretend it's your first day with our company."

Progress Review

A progress review is different from a performance review. It focuses on what's going to happen with you and the company in the next 90 days. Performance reviews tend to look in the rearview mirror. Progress reviews look out the front window. We can't do anything in the rearview mirror. That's the past. What we can make an impact on is the future.

Surveying Our Employees

Every nine months, I would have a survey distributed to all our employees, asking them how the company was doing in their eyes: what we were doing right, what we could do better. Then I would go back to them with a full report on what I had heard, what I thought was of merit, and how we would respond.

By listening to their critiques and having a system to implement changes, we gained energy and loyalty. The employees said, "This company is different from most. They really care." The survey is a great way of communicating both ways between the employees and management.

Lunch with the President

Every month, the first 10 people to sign up could come into the conference room and have a two-hour lunch with me. You could ask me any question, business or personal, and it was an open format. The communication on why the company was or wasn't doing things was frank and open. Employees found it refreshing, and it engendered loyalty.

Sharing Key Metrics and Financial Results

It's important to let employees know the results and benefits of what they've been doing. They should be informed about what is actually happening in the company. In all too many companies, particularly privately held companies, that's kept secret from people. I think if you don't realize the impact that you're making on the bottom line, there's no real reason for you to go the extra mile. Sharing the metrics and financials is a significant improvement in communication.

Senior Leadership Field Visits

I am a big fan of making sure that senior managers are out and about and not sitting behind their desk. To communicate, you need to both speak and listen, and to do so you need to be in the field with people.

Jim Koch, the founder of the Boston Brewing Company, known for its Sam Adams beer, once addressed the Inc. 500 conference and said something to this effect: "Twelve years ago, when I first started the company, I spent two days of every week calling on prospects and customers in the field with my salespeople. I'm here to tell you 12 years later I spend two days of every week in the field with my people." I think that is a terrific example of a leader actively engaging and communicating with his people.

Paul Orfalea, founder of Kinko's, grew the company from a 500-square-foot space outside the University of California, Santa Barbara, when he was a student there, into thousands of stores worldwide and sold the company ultimately to FedEx for what he calls an obscene amount of money. He says he didn't have an office at corporate. He always spent his time in the field, in the stores, visiting with the people.

There you have two very successful leaders, and both underscore how important it is to be in the field with your people.

Those, then, are 17 important steps for good communication. None is urgent. You can get by, day to day, without doing these things. But every single one is important. Company leaders are beginning to recognize that, and they are spending time cultivating good communication and other means of developing a strong corporate culture. They are paying attention to what Kotter highlighted in his study of culture-rich companies. They see what is important to accomplish, and they attend to those things. Someone else can handle those urgent matters that get in the way.

Empowerment

To truly empower your employees, you need to create an environment where the people who work in it feel comfortable making decisions, as if they were the owner.

Think of the story I told you about giving the spinach away when I was a stock boy at the grocery store. What would the store owner have done? I think he would have done what I did, and that's the environment that leaders should create, one in which employees feel comfortable playing that role.

Years ago I read a powerful book called *How to Make a Buck and Still Be a Decent Human Being* by a CEO named Rick Rose. To this day I remember his concepts on empowerment when I advise companies and speak to audiences. Rick Rose had five bullet points that he put on plastic business cards for all his employees to keep on their person, and he also put them up on big poster boards.

Here are the five points:
- Is it right for the customer?
- Is it right for our company?
- Is it ethical?
- Is it something for which you're willing to be accountable?
- Is it consistent with the company's basic beliefs?

If your answer is yes to all five questions, don't ask, just do it. If this bulletin board had been hanging up in that grocery store, and I was wondering whether to rush out for that spinach, I would just have gone through the list. Is it right for the customer to get the spinach? Yes. Is it right for the company? Yes. Is it ethical? Yes. Is it something for which I'm willing to be accountable? Yes. Is it consistent with our company's basic beliefs? Yes. Then I would know I could just get her the spinach without running around the store to ask permission.

That is a great example of empowerment. And it is yet one more way to build the kind of culture where your people are loyal and eager to do their utmost. That's what will propel your company to greater heights.

PART TWO

THINKING LIKE A COACH: THE ESSENTIALS OF SALES MANAGEMENT

CHAPTER 5

. . . .

"JOE MUST GO"

"It's not the people you fire who make your life miserable.
It's the people you don't fire who make your life miserable."
— Author Unknown

I once had a salesperson named Joe who made $40,000 a year. He worked, 100 percent, for commissions only, but in his territory he should have been making at least $100,000 a year. I told him that. "All you need to do is a half-dozen things that you're not doing," I said. "Go do those things, and you're going to be making two to three times the money that you're making today."

I went away, and three months later, I looked at his numbers, and he still had a $40,000 run rate. This time, I put it to him like this: "Let's say I owned a building and your rent was $100,000, but you were only giving me $40,000. If you didn't start paying in full, I would figure the building was too big for you. So when I see no improvement in your sales, I figure I need to cut your territory in half."

Three months later, I cut his territory in half, and Joe, on the day the new guy started, walked into my office and quit. I said, "Why are you quitting?" He said, "In that half territory, I can't live off of $20,000 a year." I shook his hand and said, "Good luck and goodbye." The next day, I came into the office, and Joe was there. I said, "What are you doing here?" He said, "Well, I talked it over with my wife, and we decided that I should work that half territory."

I thought, "Hey, this is a pretty good deal." Think about it. I don't pay him any salary. He's 100 percent commission only, and now I have two people working like that in a piece of territory that only had one before. Whatever they produce, I'm going to be ahead of the game.

The mistake is this. A nonperforming salesperson, regardless of how you pay him, at the end of the day is nonperforming. In that half territory, Joe is just going to make a mess in a smaller space. Someday, someone is going to have to come in after he has left and clean up. I would have been better off had I not had Joe in the company.

But a year later, we looked at all of the production of our salespeople. Joe made $40,000 a year. The new guy made $50,000 a year. I was right about my suspicions that we could do a lot more volume. Here's what it really taught me. I could have sliced Joe's territory into quarters. I could have sliced it into eighths. It wouldn't have mattered what size territory I gave Joe; he still would have made $40,000. That's the way it was with Joe: He woke up one day long ago and said, "It takes $40,000 to pay for what I want and need in life," and he adjusted his behavior to hit his number.

"JOE HAS TO GO"

In the 15 years that I have been working in the field with clients all over the world, in 80 industries on average per year, I have never found a business that didn't have a Joe in it. I tell my clients, "Joe has to go."

I'm a big believer in ranking our salespeople. I think we should rank our salespeople at least once a month. In ranking our salespeople, we should rank them from top to bottom.

Let's say that I had 12 salespeople. There would be three people in the top 25 percent, the top quartile. There would be three people in the second quartile, three in the third, and three in the fourth. I want to have, at least once a month, a meeting on that report with them all together, talking about those results. Some people are generating more than others are. We need to know what they are doing so that we can get the other ones to improve.

We should have one-on-one meetings, at least monthly, with those people to talk about that report. My better clients are having these one-on-one meetings on a weekly basis. I want to talk to the person who, last month, was number three out of 12 and who dropped down to number nine out of 12. My experience tells me that if you have a first-quartile person drop to the third or fourth quartile in a single month, it has nothing to do with the business. It has everything to do with what's going on in that guy's personal life. If you don't start talking about what's getting in the way in the personal life, that person could actually drop off the page and out of your company.

I want to also talk one on one to the number-10 person in your company, who jumped up in a single month to number five, and I want to find out what he or she was doing that led to that. Maybe it's

91

some things that I could teach the rest of the team to do so they can increase their production.

In summary, I'm ranking my salespeople at least once a month. I'm sharing that ranking with them at least once a month. I'm having a team meeting with them and talking about those results, and I'm having one-on-one meetings with each individual to see what's happening.

Nationwide, in all US industries combined, the bottom quartile is producing less than 6 percent of the sales. The top quartile is producing 60-plus percent. When I ask my audiences, "What do you do with this top quartile?" I hear things like this: "We praise them, we work with them, we recognize them, and we reward them." I tell them, "That's not true, guys. Of the four quartiles, tell me where you're spending the most time." They are spending the most time on the bottom.

That's right. They know what they should do, but that's not what they're doing. They figure, "Oh, those top guys, they're fine. I can leave them alone. Where I ought to spend my time is at the bottom."

Ask yourself "Where does the head coach of a sport team spend his time: first team? Second? Third?" That's right: first team. We should do the same.

DEVELOPING MINIMUM STANDARDS

In developing their sales teams, most businesses are woefully neglectful in three critical areas. We need to deal with nonproducers first. Minimum standards of performance need to be negotiated with each individual salesperson.

When I talk to those who are managing the salespeople, and I say to them, "What's the minimum standard for a salesperson to work here? What is the least amount that they can produce and still keep their job?" Sometimes the response is, "Well, we don't have anything like that." I say, "How do you manage them?" They say, in effect, "Well, we tell them to sell, please."

I go to another company, and it has 10 salespeople. All 10 salespeople have the same minimum standard. That's not much better because it's way too low for the top three guys and way too high for the bottom three. It plays to the middle.

So let me repeat: Minimum standards of performance need to be negotiated with each individual salesperson. We should not give everybody the same minimum standard. Customers should not be treated equally. Most people understand that. But it's also true that all salespeople should not be treated equally. Some should be held to a higher standard than others.

What we should be doing is customizing the minimum standard for each individual on the sales team, based upon their experience, their competencies at that time, and their territory. Some salespeople will have a higher bogey, a higher number to hit than others have. It's fair and it's equitable, based on their experience, their capabilities, and their territory.

Another key word is "negotiate." Sometimes managers go off-site, and they come up with some mumbo-jumbo numbers that the company is going to meet. They dice it up into locations. They dice it down to individual salespeople, and then they meet with their salespeople and say, "Your number is this." Well, if you don't believe in the number, then it doesn't matter. People will fight for the goals they set. It is absolutely essential that the salespeople feel ownership in their numbers.

jd

EATING WHAT THEY KILL

The closer I can get a salesperson to work on commissions only, the better I sleep at night. The further I move away from it, the more restless I am. I took on a client in Fort Collins, Colorado, who had 14 salespeople around the country, all working out of their homes. The lowest paid of the 14 had a base salary of $150,000 a year, plus quarterly and annual bonuses. Imagine what time one of those guys starts work in the morning. Maybe 10 a.m.? And then he'll have lunch at home and play with the kids, and later he'll knock off at 3 p.m., probably. I don't mind salespeople making a lot of money. In fact, I've had salespeople at my organizations with seven-figure incomes, but they ate what they killed. They were 100 percent commission-only salespeople.

SET YOUR POOR PERFORMERS FREE

If you showed me that your bottom 25 percent produced less than 6 percent while your top guys did over 60 percent, I would recommend that you set free that bottom 25 percent. Get rid of the bottom quartile. They will be good at something, but they stink at sales. And they tend to be the complainers. They're energy vampires. They talk about what they feel is bad pricing and service and all their excuses for not getting their production up. They never look at the real problem, which is them.

Most companies spend a disproportionate amount of time with their bottom-quartile employees. They're the wrong people for the job. They are a disaster when it comes to building a winning culture. When you visit a company for the first time, you can sense the culture right away. You can smell it. If you don't deal with the bottom performers, if you don't take the garbage out, your culture will stink.

Low turnover is only good among good performers. If you're not getting rid of poor performers, you not only are affecting your staff, but you also will find it extremely difficult to recruit the best. Top producers don't want to be associated with a company that tolerates poor performers and malcontents.

> *It's not the people you fire who make your life miserable. It's the people you don't fire who make your life miserable.*

In building a world-class sales organization and strong culture, first make sure you have the right people in the seats. Be deliberate. I remember hearing a speaker long ago who used four words that I still remember well: "Hire slowly; fire quickly." One of my life mentors, Jim Pratt, taught me this one: "The longest time in a manager's life is between the day you lose faith in somebody and the day you do something about it."

We need to make sure we have systems and processes to measure and report the performance of our people. Then we can take action to promote or fire. That's what makes a consistently top-performing company. That's what proactive sales managers need to do first.

It's not the people you fire who make your life miserable. It's the people you don't fire who make your life miserable.

CHAPTER 6

. . . .

RECRUITING THE TOP PERFORMERS

"Recruiting is a lot like shaving. You miss a
day and you look like a bum."
—Jackie Sherrill

I have a database of tens of thousands of people who read my newsletter. Many are salespeople. If you are a business owner or sales manager, let me ask this question: Are you presently active in the marketplace looking for someone to recruit and hire who would become your new number-one salesperson? Are you looking for a top performer?

I ask that of my audiences and, generally, fewer than half the people raise a hand. That tells me that if I came to you and said, "I've got a guy who could be your new number-one salesperson. Are you interested?" your response would be, "No, I don't want that guy." How could you not have your hand up? If you are trying to grow your company, you should always be looking for top producing salespeople.

Think of it this way. If you had 12 salespeople and I brought you a new number one, what effect would that have on your other top producers? When I ask that, people always say their sales would go up. They also agree that hiring a new number one would likely result in the hiring of other good performers.

Still, half of an audience says no to such a hire because they don't happen to be looking for anyone at the time. The first order of business is this: Recruiting is a process, not an event. It must be ongoing and continuous. To those who do raise their hand to say they are recruiting producers, I say, "Terrific! Let me see your list." They look at me blankly, as if to say, "What list?" They don't have one. And that means they are not actively recruiting.

AN IDEAL HIRING LIST

Don't expect that you will drive to your office and maybe a top producer or two will be hanging out front asking, "Are you hiring?" The only way that you can be effective at recruiting top people is to identify and go after them. That means you need a list, and it should have 10 to 15 names on it, even if you only have half that many people on your sales staff. An ideal candidate for the list is someone who is not looking for a job and is happy where he or she is currently working. That's a terrific candidate, and I'll explain why in a moment.

Suppose I gave you a choice of two candidates. One has 10 years of selling experience and worked in two companies, both in your industry, but was always in the third and fourth quartile of perfor-mance. The other candidate also has 10 years of selling experience at two companies, but none in your industry. However, he always was up in the first and second quartile of performance.

Let me guess: You would tell me that you would choose the second candidate. But if I were to go to your company, I suspect I would find that you're only recruiting inside your industry. So many business leaders strategize beautifully but execute poorly.

Open up your net. Include candidates outside your industry. You can teach a person your industry more easily than you can correct a poor producer. Yes, you want to look inside your industry, but you should also look outside it for good performers.

COURTING THE FINEST

My wife and I have been married for 44 years. We dated for four years before we got married. If we had dated only twice and then got married, we would have hurt our odds for a lasting marriage. What was integral in the success of our marriage was the courting process, getting to know each other.

As we recruit top people, we should have a courting process. You should get in touch twice a month with those 10 or 15 people on your list. It could be breakfast, lunch, dinner, ball games, industry events, an e-mail, a phone call, a personal visit. Reach out in some way about twice a month to each of them. Tell them what's happening in your company and some success stories, and catch up with what they're doing.

If you still are wondering why you need that many names on your list, here's the reason, in two words: Life happens. I don't know when those 10 or 15 people will be open to going to work for someone else. I do know that the odds are they will leave at some point, because life happens. The promotion they wanted went to somebody else.

Their industry goes into a nosedive, or their company has financial troubles and is laying people off and cutting expenses. Perhaps it is sold, and the culture changes for the worse, or the compensation methods change. Where once the people on your list were happy, they now are ready for a change. The odds are that if you are courting them twice a month, life is going to happen in the next year to one or two of those 10 or 15 people.

I have learned over many decades of recruiting that top producers tend to go where they want and when they want. They tend to go to the people who have been courting them all along the way. Top producers in sales tend to move from one industry or one company to another in what I call the still of the night. Once someone like that has made the move, people in the industry are surprised and wish they had known that he was in the job market. But the deal is done. It's too late.

That is the biggest challenge that we have. And it's the greatest opportunity. The majority of company leaders are not going after people. The only time they go after people is when they have a vacancy.

RECRUIT, DON'T ABSORB

In an organization of 12 salespeople, what do you do when your number-three salesperson walks in one day and quits? You can't persuade him to stay. You probably go back into your office and think, "I've got to get somebody, and quick." You want somebody with experience.

The trouble is this: Your prospects from other companies, those who are leaving quickly, and who have experience, albeit bad, tend to be from the bottom quartile. When you make such a hire, your

RECRUITING THE TOP PERFORMERS

customers now are dealing with a bottom-quartile guy and feel disappointed in the change. "Your company used to be good but now you sort of stink," they think.

Going after the bottom-quartile people is called absorbing people. Recruiting people is going after the top producers. People who are moving by way of Internet job board solicitations and classified ads tend to be in the lower quartiles. The top people are not looking for their next career opportunity on a job board or Internet listing. They are networking, and they are in touch with the marketplace.

DEFINE THE IDEAL CANDIDATE

You may be wondering how to find those 10 or 15 people for your list. You build what's called a position profile—not a job description, but a profile of the personal characteristics and attributes that make a good salesperson. In the workbook I use for seminars, I have a one-page profile with desirable characteristics, such as personal integrity, selling skills, people skills, goal oriented, success patterns, high achievers, sense of urgency, self-discipline.

See www.jackdaly.net for a schedule of my upcoming workshops in your area.

The way that you figure out what the good salesperson looks like is to base your profile on what your top producers look like. What are their characteristics and attributes? Once you've built this profile, put your contact information on the bottom of the profile and then carry it on your person everywhere you go. Spread the word that you are building a great company with a fun culture and that you are looking for salespeople. Explain that it doesn't matter whether they are currently in your industry. Your contacts should just send such salespeople your way, and here's what you're looking for.

Some of the best salespeople I've ever hired have been waiters and waitresses. Once, my wife and I were having dinner at a restaurant in Dana Point, California, overlooking the Pacific Ocean. Our waitress was cheery and attentive and gave us just the right amount of space.

"You're really impressive," I told her. "Is this what you aspire to do for the rest of your life?"

"No," she said, laughing. "I just use this for bringing in some money." And she told us about her college studies. She was working, going to school, dealing with a long commute, juggling responsibilities. She represented so much of what I have in the profile for a top salesperson.

I gave her a copy of that profile and my business card.

"Listen, I'm building a really cool company, and I think you would thrive in this company and you would go places. If you ever have an interest, contact me."

As we were finishing dinner, a man came up to my table and asked if we had enjoyed our meal, because he and his wife certainly had not.

"Why not?" I asked.

"Because you were talking to our waitress so much that we felt ignored."

"Well, what do you want me to do about it?" I asked. "Do you want me to pay your bill?"

"That would be a good gesture."

Sometimes recruiting can be a little bit expensive, but it's worth it if you can find people who fit. The moral of the story? Always be recruiting!

I recently arrived in Norfolk, Virginia, to give a speech. It was my first time in the airport there, and I needed to take a taxi downtown. The cabbie was remarkably personable. In fact, he was about as fine an ambassador for Norfolk as you could hope to find. In a 20-minute ride, he gave me so much information that you would think he was the president of the chamber of commerce. He talked to me about the population. He talked to me about the minor league baseball team, and he pointed out the stadium. He told me about the town's colleges.

He was in the military prior to driving his cab, he said, and he had four kids and a couple of grandkids. He told me where the two top shopping centers were in the area. I mentioned that I was a runner, and he suggested a great place to run. He told me that there was a historic church two blocks from my hotel where cannonballs from the American Civil War were embedded in the walls.

Midway to the hotel, the guy asked me if I would need anyone to return me to the airport. I told him that I was probably taken care of by my client, but he gave me his card and said if I needed somebody, he would be on call. When I got out of the cab, he again offered his service and told me to enjoy my visit.

If I were a Norfolk business owner, that's a guy I would want to consider for hire. The majority of people don't think of looking for people in all the dimensions and activities in their lives. They're missing a major component of successful recruiting—and that is to always be recruiting.

The day after I met that guy, I told an audience of about 120 entrepreneurs about him. I held up his business card and asked how many wanted his contact information. After my talk, people were standing in line to get it.

TAKE IT FROM COACH KRZYZEWSKI

My favorite college basketball coach is Coach K at Duke. Mike Krzyzewski, year after year, finds himself in the college basketball playoffs. Whether he and his team make the 64 or the 32 or the Sweet 16 or the Elite 8 or the Final 4, the guy's teams are there year after year.

Now if you were to think about Duke basketball as a business, and if you thought about the basketball players as your top sales-people, how would that work out for you? He knows he's only going to have those producers for two or three years and then they will jump ship and go to the pros. Still, year after year for decades, Duke has been in those playoffs. That's despite the annual turnover of the top producers.

The key to the Duke basketball success is that they recruit year round and at every level. They've identified kids in grade school and they're tracking them to high school and they're courting them all the way through. They're courting the parents too. Many colleges do the same. They invest a significant amount of time in the recruiting.

Compare that to businesses that don't start recruiting until they have a vacancy. If you want to build a world-class organization of top salespeople, you need to have a significant percentage of time allocated to recruiting. Imagine having 10 to 15 people on the list and then touching them with some type of breakfast, lunch, dinner, ball game, or industry event twice a month. You might recruit somebody for a year or more twice a month. That's a significant amount of time.

When you recruit on a regular, continuing basis, you are emphasizing what is important. You emphasize what is urgent when you rush to hire someone to fill a sudden vacancy. Recruiting top people needs to be a key strategy.

HOW ABOUT A FINDER'S FEE?

I ask my audiences, "How many of you have an incentive or bonus plan where you pay anybody in your company a bonus to help you find people who meet the profile of a salesperson?" Only about a fifth of the audience, at most, raise a hand.

Of those few who do pay, they tell me they pay $300, $500, $1,000, occasionally $2,000. Some don't know how much their program pays, in which case I'm betting that it's not very effective. But you can be sure that a few hundred dollars doesn't work. Fifteen years ago I offered $500 and didn't get results. I upped that to $2,000, and eventually, I said, "I'll pay anybody in the company $10,000 to help me find a person who meets the profile for a top-producing salesperson."

Some of my key executives, who had a stake in the company's profits, looked as if they were going to mutiny, so I told them to give me 15 minutes to convince them that it made sense or we wouldn't do it. I'm not suggesting that you should pay a $10,000 finder fee, but this, in essence, is what I told my people: A good salesperson in our company would do 10 deals in a month. That would be a top producer. In our company, we made $1,500 in pretax profits for every deal that came in. If I'm making $1,500 on every deal they bring in, in one month a good salesperson would have been worth $15,000 to my bottom line. In one year he would be worth $180,000. In two years, $360,000. What I was saying to my 10 direct reports is I'll pay anybody in our company a $10,000 check if that person can bring me somebody who would add $180,000 to $360,000 to my bottom line.

Why would you not write a $10,000 check to get $180,000 to $360,000 back in one or two years? Why would you not write as many as you could, starting now? And yet, to some, $10,000 is just too expensive. Let me repeat: I believe, as an entrepreneur, that there are no such things as expenses in business. There are only investments. Everything that we do in business we should review to gauge that return.

The $10,000 that I offered no longer seemed outrageous to my leadership team. We paid it in increments: $2,000 when the new person brought 10 deals to the company, another $2,000 after 20 more, and the remainder after 30 deals. That meant the $10,000 came out of a revenue stream that I wouldn't have had if the new salesperson had not come on board. The team ended up embracing the finder fee incentive. Figure out what your finder fee bonus should be.

And it clearly gave us the competitive advantage in attracting people. On the first day when a new hire started, I would present an oversized check for $10,000, made out to the employee who referred him. Even though I haven't written a dollar into the guy's hands, I present the oversized check and make a photo event out of it. We put those photos in the monthly company newsletter, along with the profile of the salesperson and a notice that we were looking for such people. We also explained the company's vision.

Imagine a company at which even someone with a $40,000 base salary could make $30,000 more in bonuses for bringing in three top salespeople. What's the culture like in that company? Is it better than the culture in yours? All we need to be is creative and active in recruiting top people. It is the key to growing a company.

THE FIVE "THREES" OF HIRING

In my experience, managers hire salespeople too quickly. They fall in love with them the first time they meet them, or they're in such need because of a vacancy that they put an offer in front of anyone who seems okay. Instead, let me suggest a formula that I call the Five Threes.

The first of the five is this: The sales manager should conduct at least three interviews with the prospective salesperson. Second, those interviews should be at three different locations. Third, the interviews should be on three different occasions. Fourth, three other people in the firm each should conduct an interview with the prospect. Fifth, repeat the process until you have three solid candidates.

That means each of those three final candidates has been interviewed at least six times. In my first interview, we might have breakfast at Denny's. If that went well, I might agree to meet back at the office in a conference room. Then we might have an interview over dinner. Why three interviews? Because each time, someone different shows up and the third interview gets closer to the real person than the first one does. During the first one, the candidates are on their best behavior, but over time, their guard comes down. After the second interview, I schedule them to meet the three others, perhaps the CEO, the head of HR, and another salesperson. I ask the three others for their observations, because they can give me perspectives beyond that of a sales manager. I then go back with their viewpoints and have my third interview with the prospect. If I complete that process repeatedly and come up with three people whom I feel good about, it's more likely that I'll choose well.

I remember again that lesson from long ago: hire slowly; fire quickly. What I find in business is very often just the opposite.

RECRUIT FOR SKILLS, HIRE FOR ATTITUDE

When you're talking about salespeople in particular, 50 percent or more of success is in their heads. Fifty percent or more of a salesperson's success has nothing to do with product, price, service, strategy, or tactics. Instead, it has to do with attitude and ambition.

As a sales manager, I can teach you product, price, service, strategies, and tactics. What I can't teach you is to get up in the morning wanting to chew raw meat off the bone. I know if I hire a guy who has that in him, I can teach him everything else he needs to know.

That's why you're likely to find good prospects working as waitresses or waiters or in many walks of life other than in your particular industry. You should be looking for someone with the right stuff. The right stuff is that personal thing.

When I'm interviewing a person, one of my favorite questions is, "Tell me when you first got into sales." A lot of the guys will answer that question by taking you right to their resume. I stop them and say, "If you're going to tell me anything that's on this resume, just stop. I can read the resume another time. I want to know if there is something else in your life that has something to do with sales."

And then I hope to hear a tale of enterprise, such as my experience as a newspaper boy at age 12. That's the kind of story that should make a sales manager take notice, whether the job is selling copiers, machinery, software, or whatever. If somebody's been at it a long time and seems to have the right stuff and attitude and work ethic, you should want to know more.

My guidance to people in the sales manager's spot is to go deep. Find the inner person. Discover things that you would never learn from the resume. You can recruit for skills, but you need to hire for attitude.

CHAPTER 7

IF YOU'RE NOT TRAINING,
YOU'RE NOT GAINING

"If your company is doing well, double your training budget.
If your company is not doing well, quadruple it."
—Tom Peters

A sales manager's job is not to grow sales. It's to grow sales-people in quantity and quality. If you do that, they in turn will grow your sales.

Recruiting is all about getting enough good people—that is, it's about quantity. Now, let's talk about how to grow the sales force in quality. That has to do with training. If you're not training, you're not gaining. What are your systems and processes to ensure that you are enhancing the skill set of your people?

There are three components of a strong training program for sales-people. The first is hands-on coaching. The second is role practice. The third we'll call the success guide. Let's take a look at each.

HANDS-ON COACHING

Too often, sales managers spend their time in their office behind their desk moving paper around. My philosophy is that the sales manager will get far better production by actively working with salespeople in the field.

There are three distinct types of calls that the sales manager can make with people in the field: the joint call, the training call, and the coaching call. Each has value, but most sales managers do none of them. If I find any sales manager out in the field making calls with the salespeople, they tend to be doing the joint call.

Let's go through and describe each one of these calls.

The Joint Call

In a joint call, the sales manager spends the day in the field with the salesperson, and then they make the sales call together. They equally participate in the call. The salesperson engages the prospect in conversation and asks questions and establishes eye contact, while the manager rides shotgun and takes notes, listening intently. But if the manager hears something that the salesperson doesn't pick up on, he jumps into the conversation and takes over, while the salesperson takes notes and listens. It's back and forth, in and out.

At the end of that call, they debrief with questions such as these: "What did you think went well there? What did you think didn't go so well there? Why were you asking that question? This is the direction I was going. What do we need to do going forward to win over the account?"

Not only is the joint call a great learning opportunity, but it is an excellent selling opportunity. The fact that the salesperson and the sales manager are out on the call together tends to mean that more

IF YOU'RE NOT TRAINING, YOU'RE NOT GAINING

business gets developed on those calls than at any other time. That's the joint call, and that's the kind, if any, that I see sales managers tend to be making.

The Training Call

In the training call, the sales manager makes the call and the salesperson rides along and takes notes, silently. The salesperson becomes the fly on the wall. The idea is to show someone else in action.

At the end of every call, we debrief. The questions go like this: "What do you do differently than I just did in there? What did you not understand? What did you like? What did you not like? When I said this, why did I say it and where was I headed? What do we need to do going forward to win over this account?" That's an entirely different call from the joint call and it's very powerful as well.

The Coaching Call

This is my favorite of the three. Very few sales managers have the courage to take this on, and when they do, they miss a key component of it. In a coaching call, the salesperson makes the call and the sales manager remains the silent observer. Sales managers who do coaching calls consistently tell me, in every industry, that these are tough.

The reason they are difficult is that it's hard to sit there silently when you see things that could be done differently. We're on a call together, and it's a coaching day. You're 40 percent through the call, and it couldn't be going better. The customer is sitting there saying, "Give me the paperwork. I'll sign whatever you want me to sign." You see those buying signals, but your leg isn't long enough to kick the salesperson, and you can't say, "Jim, just shut up. Get the deal and get out!" You cannot take over the call, and that's hard.

It's also hard when you see a really good prospect and the salesperson is blowing it from the start. It's all going badly, and you cannot take over. When I tell that to my audiences, they reply, "You dope. I'd take that call over." But let me be clear about my definition of a sales manager's job. You are there to develop the people. If you come in like a white knight, what will the salesperson do when you're not there? You weren't there to salvage previous deals, so one more lost one won't hurt that much.

Notice that on the joint call, we debriefed after every call. On the training call, we debriefed after every call. But on the coaching call, I recommend no debriefing at the end of the call. Debrief with the salesperson at the end of the day. Why? The idea is to see the pattern in the behaviors during several calls that day. If you point out areas of concern, the salesperson will keep adjusting, and it will be hard to see those patterns.

I recommend that people in sales management positions do joint calls, training calls and coaching calls and mix them up along the way. I call for a minimum of four hours a month per salesperson on those calls. If I'm a sales manager responsible for 10 people, that means 40 hours every month is devoted to that activity. No way will most sales managers spend that much time in the field with their people each month. But unless they do, they will miss the greatest opportunity to grow revenues, sales, and the company. Let me repeat: if you're not training, you're not gaining.

ROLE PRACTICE

The second component of a strong training program is role practice. For an analogy, let's turn again to the world of sports.

The better performers in sports have consistently devoted themselves to practice. When Jerry Rice, who arguably was one of the best receivers, if not the best, in all of professional football, was with the 49ers, he was known as the first guy on the practice field and the last guy to leave the practice field. When Michael Jordan played for the Chicago Bulls and they won all those world championships, he was known as the first guy on the practice court and the last guy to leave.

In pro golf, the guys who are winning a higher percentage of tournaments and a higher percentage of the money—the top 20 on the leader board—are playing in fewer tournaments. They play in fewer tournaments and they win more money and a higher percentage of the tournaments because they allocate a significant portion of their time to practice. You don't learn to get better by playing. You learn to get better by practicing. It's one of the keys to success.

In the Olympics the people who win the gold, silver, and bronze have logged a massive amount of practice to get to that medal moment.

When I ask managers where their salespeople practice, and how often, I get a blank look. The best that they come up with is, "Well, if they're practicing anywhere, they're practicing on their customers." You don't practice on real deals. You should practice inside your company to get better when you are outside your company.

During workshops, I have everybody get into groups of three. One person is going to be number one, another number two, and another number three. I designate ones as the prospects, the twos as salespeople, and the threes as observers.

"When I give you the green light," I say, "the salesperson is going to turn to the other two and tell them a lot of things, including the business you're in and the purpose of the call." Many times, when I have been out with salespeople on their calls, I ask them the purpose of what they're doing. They seem confused by the question. But how else can you know whether you're going to be a success? Never make a call without a purpose.

I ask the salespeople in my workshops to explain the type of call. Is it by phone, or in person? Is it meant to get an order, to just to build a relationship? Once that setting is established, they are going to engage in the call.

I ask the prospects to play their role realistically, not as the prospects from hell, and not as cupcakes either. Just be real, I tell them. And I tell the observers to be silent and just take notes on things they see and hear that they like and don't like and make suggestions for improvements.

After a while, I ask for feedback. Did anyone learn something that would make that person a better salesperson? All raise their hands. If you can learn something in 15 minutes, I tell them, you could do that kind of role practice with colleagues in the office or a coffee shop. It's a matter of practicing to become better players in the sport. You don't need to come to a session of mine to do this. You just have to be self-initiated and interested in improving.

I ask each person to share what he or she learned with the whole room. Then we switch hats. Number one becomes the observer, number two becomes the prospect, and number three becomes the sales person. It's an entirely new case. Then we do it a third time. It takes about an hour in all, and every time I've conducted this exercise, the groups report to me that they got consistently better. "Then let's do this three times a week for the rest of time, and imagine how good you'll be," I say.

Again, if you're not practicing like this inside your company, where are you practicing? The answer is, "I'm practicing on real deals." There isn't a sports team out there that would send players out without a lot of practice, yet many businesses hire salespeople and send them out to fend on their own. They wonder why the people aren't having success. In order to be successful you need to practice.

Rory McIlroy was named two years in a row as the golf player of the year. Last year he made a statement that he was going to cut his playing schedule down by 40 percent so that he could practice more and win a higher percentage of his tournaments and more of the majors. The people in sports get the concept of being good by practicing. Many people in business do not get it. They continue to rush to the urgent, failing to invest in the important—and practice is highly important.

To illustrate another lesson from the exercise, I ask the participants, "You wore the hat of a salesperson, of a prospect, and of the observer. Which hat did you wear when you learned the most?" All group members tell me the same thing. They learned the most as the observer, because the other two people were in the heat of the action.

My recommendation here is this. Model the masters. If I were hired by a company to be a salesperson and the company had 100 salespeople in it, I would negotiate with the sales manager to not expect any production from me in my first 30 days. What I would want is permission in my first week to go out with the number-one salesperson in the company, in the second week with number two, and in the third week with number three.

I would find out how they managed time, how they kept in touch with prospects and kept them in the pipeline to become clients, what their key activities were like, and why they did what they did. What were the top five things I should focus on to excel at this job? What were the top five to avoid? I'm going to find out all that the top three people have learned over their career that enables them to be in the top quartile.

After all, it's the people in the top quartile who win those trips and accolades, year after year. What that tells me is that they are doing something entirely different with the same product, service, and price. Instead of telling the sales force to "go make a bunch of calls, knock on doors, ring the phone, the more calls you make the better, blah, blah, blah," wouldn't it make much more sense to practice and then to get them teamed up with the top people and let them learn from them? I often hear comments such as this from people who have done the exercise in my workshops: "This role practice makes a ton of sense. I'm going to do this regularly from now on."

THE SUCCESS GUIDE

For training your salespeople, we have come up with a success guide with the most effective techniques that top producers use and that others should emulate. The success guide starts with a simple concept: there's hardly anything that goes on in a sales call that couldn't be anticipated.

One of the things that we have seen is that the top-performing salespeople are canned. They say the same thing in the same way each time they encounter a particular situation. When they call on a prospect who says, "I'm already happy doing business with the XYZ Company," and they hear that four times from four different people during the day, the better salespeople have no hesitation. They respond confidently, quickly, and consistently, the same way every time, because they have figured out what works.

The beauty of the top people is that their responses sound as though they are saying them for the very first time. They never sound canned. Let's put it this way. Suppose I bought tickets for a couple hundred dollars each to Phantom of the Opera on Broadway. The show has been on Broadway for years, eight shows a week, but it's the first time for me. So that night I don't want the cast feeling they are tired of saying the same stuff and wanting to make up some new stuff. What I want those people behind that curtain to be feeling is this: "We're going to deliver our lines as if it's opening night."

Every call is opening night for the best salespeople. They are canned but don't sound canned. They don't sound like a telemarketer reading from a script. They are professionals who practice and are consistent in using the approach that works.

In building this success guide, we tried to anticipate things that would improve sales calls and how to better prepare. One is the objection guide. Visit **www.leveragesalesmgmt.com** to learn more about the success guide.

When I ask audiences how many objections a prospect can come up with, they say it's just about infinite. I tell them that there are no more than 15. I offer to take my entire audience to the bar for free drinks if they can come up with more than 15 in an hour. I give them five to begin with and write them on the whiteboard: "The price is too high." "I'm happy doing business elsewhere." "I had a bad experience with your company once." "I'm looking for a national company, not a local one." "I'm looking for a wider array of choices."

I ask the audience to supply the remaining 10. I've never had to buy the cocktails. It's a legend that there are an infinite number of objections. There are 15 at most and, for many businesses, fewer than 10. It would make sense for a company and its salespeople to figure out what those are and then work at coming up with the best response or two for each. Still, 99 percent of companies have not taken the time to do so.

Most salespeople wing it. They throw stuff at the wall to see if it will stick. When I go out in the field with a third-quartile salesperson, he will have three responses for three people who say they're already happy doing business with somebody else. They try something different when their previous effort failed to get a deal. But when I go out with the top people, they take the same approach every time. They anticipate the major objections, and they are prepared with a response.

After identifying those objections and preparing the responses, you need to figure out the best questions to ask. If the responsibility for a good salesperson is to ask better questions, then why not brainstorm, as a sales group, on what those questions should be, and practice them?

I'm convinced that whenever a salesperson calls on someone, that person has an ultimate question that often goes unasked. That question is: "Why should I do business with your company?"

In my live sessions I pick a company that is represented in my audience and ask those salespeople to stand in front of the room. "What does your company do?" I ask.

"Well, we sell tools for builders," one of them might respond.

"Great," I say, "so why should I do business with your company?"

"Lots of products," one salesperson responds. "Good quality," says another, and the next one says, "Experience." Then I hear, "Knowledgeable." And, "We care about you." And, "We're national in size." It goes on. I write all those answers on the board.

I then turn to the audience. "Let's say that I pick a competitor of theirs," I say, and I ask a group from a competing company to stand. "Why should I choose your company?" I ask. Would they tell me they have good service? Would they tell me they're experienced? Would they tell me they're knowledgeable?

Every time I do this exercise, the salespeople offer me nothing unique, nothing differentiated. They give me the same stock answers. They're just throwing stuff against the wall.

If you, as a salesperson, don't know how to differentiate your company from anyone else's out there, then how will I, as a possible buyer of your service, be able to pick you over someone else?

The best resource I have ever found to prepare people to answer the question of why I should do business with your company is a book by Jaynie Smith called *Creating Competitive Advantage*. What she would tell you and what I would tell you is that your statement should be unique, specific, and detailed. It should be a response that your competitors would not likely offer.

Once you have that response, put it on your website and collateral materials, and make sure your salespeople practice it until it flows like melted butter off their tongues. I have such a statement on my business card and website and in my workbooks. It has several bullet points that are so unique and specific that any competitor in my sales and speaking space would find them hard to match.

I talk about leading sales forces numbering in the thousands. I talk about being TEC Australia Speaker of the Year, and Vistage UK Overseas Speaker of the Year. I mention that I built six companies from scratch, international firms, and that I worked with a company as a partner and owner that was tenth on the Inc. 500, and was a winner of the Entrepreneur of the Year honors from Ernst and Young. I have a bachelor's in accounting and a master's in business. I was an army captain. The statement leaves people thinking, "Jack Daly produces results. This guy speaks from experience."

What I would tell any of my prospects is: "If you're going to choose somebody other than me to do your sales training for you, I want to meet that guy because he's got to be something else."

I worked hard on those bullet points. I met and worked with Jaynie Smith. I devoured her book and I now tell all my audiences to read that book. Your salespeople need to be clear and respond automatically to "Why should I choose your company?" They should be ready to answer any objections and know the

> *I once heard it said this way: "When you fly by the seat of your pants, expect turbulence!"*

right questions to ask. They should know the features and benefits of each of your products. They should be ready to provide success examples and testimonials from people who underscore that you deliver on the goods.

If a company were to take seriously this success guide and build upon it, sales could increase 20 percent or higher. Nonetheless, the overwhelming majority of companies don't invest the effort. It's not considered urgent. Once again, we see that poor choice of the urgent over the important. I once heard it said this way: "When you fly by the seat of your pants, expect turbulence!"

PART THREE

BIRTH OF A SALESMAN:
LEARNING TO SELL TO ANYBODY

CHAPTER 8

. . . .

BE MEMORABLE

"The key is good communication. People are
down on what they are not up on."
— Author Unknown

A good first impression is essential to sales success, and getting off to a favorable start with your prospects isn't difficult if you employ some simple tactics. Keeping your voicemail greeting relevant and updated daily is the first one, and another is what I call your "moneybag," filled with tools to help you bring in the profits.

In this chapter, we'll take a look at both. Just as company leaders must communicate the corporate vision to employees, an individual salesperson must keep in touch with prospects and customers in a way that they will not soon forget. The key is good communication. People are down on what they are not up on.

YOUR DAILY GREETING

It's hard to imagine a business without phones, and every sales-person uses voicemail. But when I ask how many salespeople change that voicemail greeting every day, I find that only a very few do. So what happens when a salesman spends the day at a seminar and can't take calls? What does that communicate to prospects about his or her availability?

A major frustration among customers is that they don't know when the salesperson might get back to them. They hear a voicemail message that the salesperson recorded when he or she first got the phone. It says something like this: "Your call is important to me. I'm either away from my desk or on the other line. Please leave a message and I'll get back to you." Everyone else's message sounds like that too. It's boring and gives no indication to your callers when or if you're going to call them back. And in fact, with the high job turnover lately, the person who recorded the message might have left without erasing it.

That's why we recommend that you change your voicemail greeting every day, and in doing so you can demonstrate to callers that you are attentive to their needs. "Hi, this is Jack Daly and it is Wednesday, June 26th and I'm at a sales workshop where I hope to get ideas to better serve you, my customers. I'll be checking my messages and return your call promptly. Meantime, have an awesome day."

That's far better than what callers have come to expect. Such a message reassures the customers that the greeting is timely and that they will get a response. Salespeople have told me that when they start doing this, callers leave messages of appreciation for the thoughtful-ness. You can make your daily greeting unique. One salesman, a big sports fan, includes the scores of a couple of the previous night's games. Another offers the local weather forecast. And another tells you which celebrities are celebrating their birthday that day. You can do so much more than merely say that you're away from your desk or on another line.

IMMEDIATE FOLLOW-UP

Let me tell you about my "moneybag." It's a simple tactical tool, or set of tools, and I call it that because it has made me seven figures of income in my life as a salesperson. You can have a moneybag, too. Think of the kind that stores use for bank deposits and fill with cash and checks. I have some different things inside mine, things that will produce that cash and those checks in abundance.

Inside my moneybag are my company-issued thank-you cards and envelopes and a stack of my business cards. Those are important tools for anyone's moneybag, but I also have tools in there that I hope will make me really stand out as memorable for my prospects and clients.

One is a blue felt-tip pen. I use a blue pen because people often tell me I have brilliant blue eyes and I figure they'll associate blue with me. Pick your own color and style, and in time, your public will see it as your brand.

I also have stamps in my moneybag, but my stamps are unique. Some show me in a business suit. Others show me crossing a finish line with the words "Ironman Jack" printed on them. You can buy personalized stamps over the Internet. You can get them from stamps. com or zazzle.com.

My moneybag also contains specialized photo cards and envelopes. I purchased my photo cards from Shutterfly.com, which I have used for years although I'm sure there are other vendors. The cards are blank inside for notes, but the fronts show photographs of me in a variety of settings. Some show me golfing in full kilt attire in Ireland. I send those to the golfers I meet as thankyou cards. Inside, I write something like, "Rick, it was a pleasure meeting with you, and I'm excited that doing business with you will be a win/win. But I'm even more excited that we share a passion for golf, so let's get together soon on the course. Thanks, Jack." If I were dealing with an avid fisherman, I'd send a card showing me shoving off from Cabo San Lucas and I would write that we should go out for some marlins sometime. I have a marathon card, a dancing card, a triathlon card, and a card showing my grandsons, Malcolm and Wyatt. I have a card showing me gambling, and one at the Playboy mansion at poolside.

I'm looking for any hook that I can when I'm making a call with you so that we can bond. That's the whole idea of the moneybag. I'm finding ways to stand out from everyone else. To do well in sales or in any pursuit, you need to be unique and memorable.

Here's what I do when I encounter someone new. Somewhere along the line, we exchange business cards. As soon as possible— sometimes I'm still sitting in my car in the parking lot, or in a chair in the hotel lobby—I take a moment and enter all of the information from the business card into my database, using my iPhone or whatever I'm packing with me. I don't even need to use a keyboard. Using an app called CardMunch, I can take a photograph of the card with my iPhone and the app populates everything on the card into my database. I then write an e-mail, thanking the prospect for meeting with me and confirming what we agreed would happen next, who's going to do what, and by when.

I send that e-mail while still in the lobby or parking lot. The timing is essential. One of the raps that salespeople get is that we're not proactive communicators. Sending an e-mail so quickly sends a strong signal to prospects that you're on the ball now and imagine how much you'll be on the ball when you do business together. I want the prospect to compare my way of doing things with the way my competition probably has been doing things. That's why the immediacy of the e-mail is key.

The contents of the e-mail, then, should clearly communicate two things. It should express my gratitude for the person's time, and it should confirm the next step. Always create a next action step at the end of a sales call. That way, the next time you meet you can pick up where you left off. If you don't create an action step, then you will find yourself starting all over, and that's no way to gain the momentum you need to reach the finish line.

While I'm still in the lobby or the parking lot, I take out my moneybag. From the conversation I've had with the prospect, I know something about what he or she enjoys in life. Choosing an appropriate photo card, I write a thank-you note, mentioning something we could do together socially. Then I choose a personalized stamp to mail it. For a formal organization, I'll use a stamp showing me in a suit and tie. But if the prospect was impressed by my marathons, I'll use one of my Ironman Jack stamps.

KEEPING IT PERSONAL

And when I address the envelope, I write "Personal" next to the name before dropping the note in the nearest mailbox. That's something that we learned from the top 10 percent of performers out there in sales. No matter what industry we work with, it seems the better salespeople actually call on fewer people and they write more business. The key is they call on the right people. They call higher up in the organization. The higher up they can call, the bigger and easier the sale tends to be.

That's because they are dealing with a person with a broader array of responsibility. He or she has the ability to open several channels of business for you, instead of just the one channel you were dealing with lower in the organization. And that person has more authority and can get approvals more readily, which makes it easier for the salesperson. If the salesperson can reach the top person, the decision could come immediately. The lower people in the organization, the ones whom most of the third- and fourth-quartile producers in sales tend to deal with, are not empowered. They have to go through a series of approvals, which slows the sale, and their limited responsibility means the sale size is smaller.

As the top producers reach higher up, however, they more often run into personal assistants. One of the jobs of personal assistants is to sort the mail for the boss. They throw out the junk mail and then make a stack. At the bottom of the stack are newspapers and magazines; next up are activity reports; next up is correspondence, and at the very top of the pile are things noted as personal.

That means my thank-you card is going to be on the top of the pile the day after the sales call. They already have gotten that immediate e-mail from me, and then the very next day they get a handwritten card, which gets them to thinking, "Wow, this guy is really on top of his game. I'm going to take a serious look at possibly shifting some business his way."

Here's how it once worked out for me. I was called in to a major company based in Pittsburgh, Pennsylvania. I met for an hour with the CEO of the company and three vice presidents, and then we exchanged business cards. In the parking lot, I entered all of their data into my database. I sent them each an e-mail individually, not a group message, because each person has a different perspective and the notes have to be tailored to the personality. Then I wrote four handwritten cards, each marked "Personal," and mailed them.

Three months later, I was in Pittsburgh in a hotel ballroom with 175 sales reps from all over North America brought in by that company. As he introduced me, the CEO said he had only met me three months earlier.

"Let me tell you a story," he told the audience. "We met for an hour, and I went back to my desk. Soon I hear my computer go 'ding' to tell me I had an incoming e-mail. It was from Jack Daly, but how could that be? He'd have to still be in the building. My head of sales, who had been at the meeting too, also had gotten an e-mail from Jack. Everyone at the meeting got one. And the very next day, we each got a handwritten note. That's when I said, "Call that guy up and see when he's available. We're taking 175 reps, we're going to put them in a ballroom, and we're going to spend the day with that guy. If the only thing they learn is how he did that, it'll be worth our time and his fee."

That company hired me on four additional occasions to speak. It passed me on to two of its clients and paid for that as a value-add for them, and then hired me for four, quarterly, webcast, one-hour productions to sell with the company's best customers. And that all resulted from what was in my moneybag. Until I met with them, none of them had known me.

That's why you need a moneybag. It's very tactical and it works wonders, as many have attested after coming to my sessions. It's simple, just as changing your voice message greeting each day is simple, but sometimes the simplest strategies are the most effective in putting you far ahead of your competitors.

....

See www.jackdaly.net for my current workshop schedule.

....

If salespeople were going to work in my company, I'd require these things: They must change their voicemail greeting daily, and they must use their moneybag. In fact, I have clients who give their salespeople moneybags imprinted with the company name and logo, telling them that using the moneybag isn't an option; it's the way they will do business. It's a system and a process that works.

CHAPTER 9

. . . .

THE CRITICAL PATH TO SUCCESS

"People without leaders are lost, but leaders
without process are doomed."
—Frank Pacetta

I f you could reduce a course on sales to the shortest lesson possible, it would be summed up in one four-word sentence: "Ask questions and listen." If you make sales, you can make a living, but if you make an investment of time and good service in a customer, you can make a fortune. That is the essence of the critical path to success.

I illustrate this path with a pyramid, at the base of which is foundational information that a salesperson must

> If you make sales, you can make a living, but if you make an investment of time and good service in a customer, you can make a fortune.

jd

communicate to a prospect, and rising to a pinnacle of action steps. This path, if followed faithfully, leads to deals aplenty.

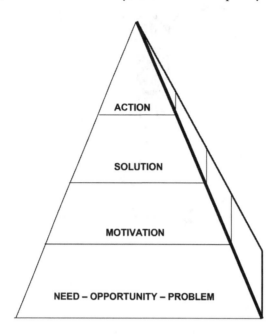

Many people get into sales because they're good on their feet, and they like interacting with others. They go out into the marketplace and do what they think they do best. They show up and then they throw up. They yak-yak-yak-yak, and figure if they just talk enough, somebody will buy this stuff. They fancy themselves so engaging. But it's better to be interested than to be interesting. Let the prospect take center stage.

"No one ever lost a sale by listening too closely," says noted entrepreneur and engineer Robert Epstein. Your success as a salesperson is not related to your ability to give information but rather, to your ability to get information.

The reality of sales is that people do not want to be sold. I've never met anyone who enjoys having someone try to sell them something.

> It's better to be interested than to be interesting. Let the prospect take center stage.

So my first directive to salespeople when it comes to selling strategies is to quit selling. It doesn't work, and no one likes it.

When I tell that to my audiences, people look at me as if to say, "What the heck am I supposed to do? I'm a sales guy." And I tell them to change the definition of selling. My favorite is to help them to buy. The subtle difference between selling someone something and helping them to buy is profound.

SELLING BY HELPING

That puts us at the bottom of the pyramid. Help them with their needs; help them with their opportunities; help them with their problems; help them get to their destination; help them be more successful.

In some businesses, a salesperson's job can be articulated as "help them make more money." If you help your customers with their needs, opportunities and problems, they tend to give you the business, but first, you have to know what those needs, opportunities, and problems are. And the only way you're going to find that out is by asking more questions.

And so our recommendation is that 50 percent of a salesperson's time should be spent at the base of the pyramid asking more questions. The top 10 percent of salespeople are asking six questions for every one that the average performer is asking. The message that we have for salespeople is this: The person who asks the questions is in control.

IF THEY TRUST YOU, THEY'LL BUY FROM YOU

So many salespeople think they need to push, shove, and manipulate. In reality, what they need is to develop a trusted partner relationship, helping customers with their needs, opportunities, and problems. In fact, one of a salesperson's best initial moves might even be to send the prospect to someone else who can better solve the problem.

Let me give you an example. About twice a month, I am contacted by sales managers and business owners asking me if I can help them design a new compensation plan for their salespeople. Years ago I built some comp plans for my own company and for some clients. But I discovered I'm not really good at that. There are people way better at comp plan design than I am. In my database I have three trusted resources on comp plan design. That's all they do. And if you were to go to them, they'd get it to you quicker, better and cheaper than I could.

Each of those calls could mean money for me. I could register a sale. I could put the money in my pocket, and yet I'm saying no. Go down the street to that other guy. Never once has anyone come back to me to say, "No, Jack, we want you to do it." My referral satisfied all of them.

And six months or two years later, I'm likely to get a call back from that person who had wanted me to design a compensation plan. I hear this: "Jack, we want to hire you to do sales training." Perfect! That's what I do. And we make it happen. How many other firms do you think that person talked to about doing sales training for his company? Zero. They trusted me.

Here is a critical message for any salesperson to understand: Selling is the transfer of trust. People do business with people they trust. I could have done the comp plan design. They would not have known they could have gotten it quicker, cheaper, and better somewhere else. But I would have known, and I would have violated my definition of good selling, which, again, is to help my clients with their needs, opportunities, and problems in the best way that I can—and here's the key part—even when it means not directly employing me. Because when it is my turn, they will come to me and they won't be shopping me with someone else. They won't be measuring me, or my price, against others, because I created the base of trust.

Trust trumps price. If you are running into price objections frequently in your business, it would suggest to me that one of two things, or both, are not going well for you: either you have not created enough trust—and the way you create trust is to care more about the customer than you do about your sale—or you have not created the perceived value that overcomes price objections. More on perceived value later.

PURSUING CENTERS OF INFLUENCE

While we're still at the base of the pyramid, I want to also share one other strategy that brings great success. That is what I will call pursuing centers of influence. Sometimes your best customers will never, ever buy your product or service. But they could bring you a windfall of business.

Here's an example. When I got into the triathlon sport, I didn't know how to swim, so I took swim lessons from a renowned US coach. Eventually I told my coach that I needed to spend fewer hours with him and more time on the bike. In response, my coach told me about a good place to buy a bike. He sent me to some nondescript industrial building. It had no signs, and no traffic rolled by. I never would have found that shop without his referral. I introduced myself to the owner, Hank, telling him my swim coach Steve had sent me over. Hank ended up selling me a bike after spending two hours with me, asking me many questions about the bike, the fit, how I would be using it. He had me check out several bikes and sent me out for test drives on a couple of them. He sent me home with a bike to try out for a few days. It was an incredible experience. I didn't know at that point whether I was going to buy that bike from Hank, but I did know that when I decided to buy a bike, I would buy it from him. He took the time to figure out what was best for me. He cared about my needs.

One strategy for a bike shop owner could be to spend a lot of money on marketing and a lot of money on the building and on signage. He could have a building on the freeway with a big sign, and he could spend a fortune on marketing. Still, it's hard to find potential bike buyers like Jack Daly among the masses.

Another approach for a bike shop owner could be to build a strong relationship with 10 swim coaches in his geographic marketplace. He also could build a strong friendship with 10 bike coaches. You could build a strong relationship with 10 trainers in the fitness centers, and 10 nutritionists.

Now that's 40 people, in four categories, and those people could send you a steady stream of business and you could locate in a cheaper area without the marketing and other expenses. I would classify those 40 people as centers of influence. In your own business, your challenge is to identify those strategic centers of influence who are so often overlooked by your competitors because they're not directly buying the product or service.

My swim coach never bought a bicycle from Hank, but the amount of business he was able to send to Hank because of that relationship and friendship was enormous. I can attest to that. I sent someone whom I met while swimming laps to Hank's triathlon shop to buy a wetsuit. I told him it was a great place in a nondescript industrial park. Later, Hank thanked me for sending the guy over and said he not only bought a wetsuit but was out road-testing a $7,500 bike.

The significant amount of business that centers of influence can send you is an example of leveraging your time and effort. Remember, the better salespeople are calling on fewer people, but they're calling on the right ones and writing more business. When you come by way of referrals, you tend to be less price sensitive because you already trust the person who sent you.

To learn more, I recommend *Getting Naked* by Pat Lencioni. It's a story-based book, with no technical jargon whatsoever. He tells how to build business with the kind of relationships that I've been describing. The essence of *Getting Naked* and of what I've been talking about here is this: When you care

> *Two people who want to do business together won't let the details keep it from happening. If two people don't want to do business together, the details won't let it happen.*

more about the customer than you do about the sale, you will sell more than anyone else out there.

Most salespeople only care about getting the deal. That's not the way to make a career out of selling. The way to make a career out of selling is by building trusted relationships and helping your clients. Even if they go elsewhere, when it is your turn, they'll come to you and only to you, and your business will be bigger and richer. Two people who want to do business together won't let the details keep it from happening. If two people don't want to do business together, the details won't let it happen.

Thanks for that one, Jim Pratt!

WHAT MOTIVATES THE BUYER?

On every call, whether it's over the phone or in person, I ask myself what will motivate my prospect to do business with me? And "motivation" is the next level up on the critical path to success.

The short answer is this: People will do business with you if they like you. If they don't like you, they won't do business with you. Top-producing salespeople ask, "How can I get this person to like me quicker and better than my competitor?" The way that they do that is by selling to the prospect's personality.

In other words, the very best salespeople don't sell to everybody the same way. They're like chameleons, and they morph into being more like the person they're calling on. They know that people tend to like people who act more like them.

And so what you should figure out is what type of person you are calling on, and then adjust your style to be more reflective, understanding, and accommodating to that individual. Let's take a closer look at how to figure out a person's personality, do it in quick order, and then adjust to be more reflective of that personality.

ADJUSTING TO PERSONALITIES

People do things for their own reasons, and they accept a salesperson's ideas not so much because they fully understand those ideas but because they feel understood. We all know that people are different, and we adjust to their personalities intuitively, but let me suggest that we can do it more effectively.

The first time you call on someone, there is high tension, but if you call the same person 10 times, the tension subsides. On the first call, the level of trust is low, but it's higher after 10 calls. Nobody buys things in a high-tension, low-trust environment. Where people buy is in a high-trust, low-tension environment, and we need to figure out how to get people there.

We designed a system that a salesperson can use to figure out a basic personality type in less than two minutes, even over the phone with someone new. How can you gauge all that so quickly? The key is to listen for it.

People tend to fall into one of four basic personality types that psychologists recognize. Two are assertive types: "expressive" or "driver." Two are nonassertive: "amiable" or an "analytical." Our model adopts those types but makes the process simple for use in sales.

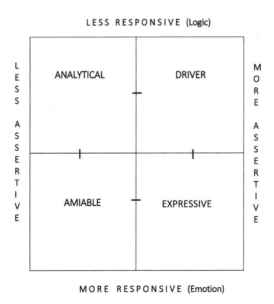

LESS RESPONSIVE (Logic)

	LESS ASSERTIVE		MORE ASSERTIVE
	ANALYTICAL	DRIVER	
	AMIABLE	EXPRESSIVE	

MORE RESPONSIVE (Emotion)

To help identify your prospect's particular personality type, you can ask yourself two key questions. The first is this: "Is this person more assertive or less assertive than the typical person that I do business with?" I ask my audiences how they see me, and they say more assertive. That assessment narrows my personality type to two possibilities.

The second question is how the prospect tends to make decisions. Are the decisions based mostly on logic, or on emotion? My decisions tend toward the logical.

Highly assertive people who make decisions based on logic are drivers, and that's me. Those whose decisions are based on emotion are expressives. Less assertive people who make decisions logically are analytics. Less assertive people who make decisions emotionally are amiables.

Each of us developed one of these four personalities by the age of 13, based upon our genetic makeup and how we were raised. Once we've established our personality, it stays with us the rest of our lives. Of the people you meet, 75 percent statistically have a different personality type than you. If you sell to everybody as if that person were the same as you, three quarters of the time you will get off on the wrong foot. Top salespeople figure out the personality type of their prospects, and they adjust their own accordingly.

Analyticals—the less assertive, logical decision makers—are technician type people. They dot their i's, they cross their t's, they do things by the book. Sometimes they even write the book that others live by. They are cautious and precise and detail-oriented.

If you are a salesperson with an analytical personality, and you were selling me that way, I would feel as if you were burying me in details. I couldn't wait to get away from you, because you wouldn't be selling to me the way I appreciate.

If you are selling to analyticals, your biggest challenge is that they are slow to make decisions because they tend to need more information. Don't try to rush them. The calls will take longer. The whole sales process will take longer.

When my audiences take into account that I'm very serious about my goals and have a system and a process for most everything, and that I was an accountant and a CPA, they will recognize that I make decisions based on logic more than emotion. That and my assertive style are what make me a driver. Another word for driver is control. These people are very often decision makers and leaders of businesses. They say, "Give me a goal and get out of the way; I'm going to go make it happen."

The biggest challenge in calling on these people is that they are blunt and direct. If you want to be more effective as a salesperson, when you're calling on a driver, be blunt and direct. They will respect you more for it.

Amiables are one of the two nonassertive types. Another word for amiable is supportive. They are kind, warm, gentle, and will go out of their way to help you. They are the salt of the earth. The challenge in selling to amiables is that they won't tell you what they really think. They don't like confrontation. You may think the sales call is going well—after all, you hear no objections—but after you leave, the prospect will tell a friend he'll never do business with you because he just doesn't like you. But an amiable type will rarely tell you straight up.

Assertive people who make decisions emotionally are the expressives. Another word for expressive is social, outgoing. These are the life of the party, the creative types, the "people" people. They'll ask if you have heard this joke, and when you say yes you have, they will tell you the joke anyway. "Hey, you haven't heard me tell it,"

143

the expressive will say. "I will tell it better." These are fun, creative, outgoing people.

Seventy percent of the people in sales tend to be expressives. The biggest challenge with the expressive is that, of the four types, they are the worst listeners. That is crucial to understand: The key to sales is to ask questions and listen, yet 70 percent of the people doing that job are the worst listeners. If salespeople could only take that outgoing, "we all love you" personality and get their ears to work too, they would thrive.

The hardest challenge is selling to someone who is different from you both in level of assertiveness and in the manner of making decisions. Analyticals and expressives have a hard time selling to each other and doing business with each other, likewise for the amiables and drivers. The amiables think the drivers are mean, and the drivers think amiables are cupcakes. An analytical thinks an expressive is a BS artist, as in "Every time I ask for proof and documentation, he offers me game tickets and a beer." Yet the expressive looks at the analytical and thinks, "My, he is so anal. He's way too detailed. "

Once you recognize your own personality traits and the fact that most other people are different from you, you can adjust your style during a sale to reflect the prospect's personality.

The Platinum Rule by Tony Alessandra is a classic book for salespeople that deals with these personality types. He writes that we all know the golden rule—that we should treat others the way we would like to be treated—but the platinum rule is to treat people the way they want to be treated. Adjust your style to be more compatible with theirs.

After you recognize your prospect's style, make a note in your database next to his or her name. That way you can look it up later: "Ah, Jack Daly is a driver, so I'll be like a driver when I talk to him."

And if the sales person ever leaves the company, the new salesperson will have that personality profile at his fingertips. It will be part of a system and process, ready to be leveraged at all times by the company.

PRESENTING YOUR SOLUTION

Moving up the pyramid on that critical path to success, the next section is "Solution." To most salespeople, that means telling the prospect, "Here is what we can do for you." But that's short of the mark.

Right before you get to that "action" pinnacle of the pyramid, which I call AFB, or asking for the business, you do need to indicate that what you are selling is a solution for the prospect, but here is a better way to articulate it: "Here is what we can do for you, and this is how you will benefit. And based upon these benefits, are we now ready to move forward with this?" In most businesses, people do not care how you do what you do. The only thing they care about is how they are going to benefit.

Salespeople should spend a lot less time talking about the specifics of their products and their services, spend a lot less time on the ego of their company, and spend more time in the shoes of the buyer and articulate the deal from the buyer's vantage point. How, based upon this product or service, are they going to benefit?

This is a big shortcoming in sales training. Too many companies train their salespeople by teaching them, at great length, all the intricacies of the product or the service, and then they set them loose on the marketplace. And after the salespeople learn all those intricacies, they feel compelled to puke them all over their prospects. Again, buyers don't care how it's done. Buyers care how they will benefit.

And that ends my synopsis on moving upward on the pyramid of sales success. Remember that it all started with a simple lesson distilled to a few words: "Ask questions and listen." That is the essence of professional selling. You're not learning anything when you're talking. Now, let's move on to look at the systems and processes that make us better at climbing that pyramid.

> You're not learning anything when you're talking.

CHAPTER 10

· ·

BACKWARD THINKING

"If you want to be a big company tomorrow, you
have to start acting like one today."
—Thomas J. Watson Jr.

"Begin with the end in mind" is how Stephen Covey phrased the concept that I call "backward thinking." Each of us needs to come up with our individual definition of success, and then set out on a course that will get us there. As a salesperson, you can't get to your destination unless you know what your destination is.

There are four key components of backward thinking. If any one of these four parts is missing, the likelihood that you will achieve success as a salesperson is severely hampered.

jd

PUT YOUR GOALS IN WRITING

The first is that your goals must be in writing. If your goals are not in writing, they're dreams. Dreams don't often come true, but goals in writing do. So the first measure of a successful salesperson is putting those goals in writing. However, that is just the first component; if you miss the next three, you still probably are not going to achieve the goals.

So many of us seem so earnest when we make those New Year's resolutions, which we may or may not put in writing. A common one is "Be healthy, join fitness club." As a result, fitness club regulars like me hate going to the club in January because of all those people coming because of that resolution. By February, they're all gone, and you don't see them the rest of the year. The reason is they didn't put together line items two, three, and four. They only worked on the first part. The lesson for salespeople is this: Don't be like that January visitor to the gym. If you want to produce results all year long, then you need to do more.

A WRITTEN PLAN WITH SPECIFIC ACTIVITIES

The second component to success through backward thinking is to have a written plan on how you're going to achieve your goals. The key is to include specific activities in that plan. If I were to give a salesperson a simple formula for selling success, it would be to first identify and then perform the activities necessary to generate sales for his or her particular business.

If the first part of that formula is to identify the activities and the second part is to do them, then the third part is to reap the rewards. Any time that I'm hired by a client to come in and try to figure out why some of the salespeople are getting the job done and others aren't, I just go to that formula and find the poor performers either haven't identified the activities or, in most cases, simply aren't regularly doing them.

The top 10 percent of performers in sales are focused on the activities. They will not go home on any given night without finishing those activities. It is the absolute key to their

> *If you are going to lose your job, be sure it's for what you did, not for what you didn't do.*

success. Those who perform in the middle of the pack or below will come up with a variety of reasons for not getting to the activities. Top producers, by contrast, are unrelenting. If making 50 phone calls a day has been identified as crucial to meeting goals, the top people won't go home without getting 50 done. The mediocre to poor performers will do 15 to 20 and say, "I can't take it anymore; let me come up with some other activities that I can work on." So they'll file an expense report, nice and tidy, and do other things that don't generate sales.

By contrast, the top people are focused on activities, and I can't underscore that enough. If you are going to lose your job, be sure it's for what you did, not for what you didn't do.

THINGS THAT GET MEASURED GET DONE

The third component of backward thinking is a system of measurement. As a sales manager working with a salesperson, I would ask this first: "What is your sales goal for this year?" Let's say that you told me your goal was a million dollars in sales. The first thing to do is to stress-test that number. Is it reasonable? Too high, or too low?

Does it have stretch in it, but not so much stretch that it'll break you? I'm going to really push hard on whether that's a real, solid number.

Let's say that I'm comfortable with that million bucks. The next thing I'm going to ask you to do is break it down into months: How much is going to be done in January? In February? You tell me $100,000 of the million is going to get done in January. I then would want you to break your months into weeks. You tell me that the first week you're going to do $30,000; the second week, $20,000; the third week, $30,000; and the fourth week, $20,000.

Once we get to your weekly targets that add up to a million dollars in 52 weeks, then I ask you to write down the activities necessary to generate that million in sales. Every industry has a unique list of activities, and a leader needs to figure out what those are. The best way to do that is to interview top producers and observe their activities, because, clearly, whatever they're doing generates results.

I would want to know how much of that $30,000 in the first week is going to come from existing customers, how much from new customers, and how much from referral business? The referral business is often the highest margin of those three categories and the least price sensitive. But it is a rare day indeed that I run into any organization or any salesperson with a targeted goal of referral business.

I have learned that if you write down a goal and measure whether you're getting it done, you will generate much more. Things that get measured get done, clearly. I might want to know, under key activities, how many outbound calls you will need for that $30,000. I might want to know the number of inbound calls needed, and the number of face-to-face appointments and presentations. How many networking events will you have that week? How many trade shows and personal marketing initiatives? The list could go on, but the point is that every business has a unique list and we need to figure it out.

A SYSTEM OF ACCOUNTABILITY

The fourth and final component of thinking backward to your goal is accountability. At the end of every week, as your sales manager, I would require you to tell me what you actually accomplished with every activity. How many outbound calls? How many inbound? How many presentations? How much face-to-face time? That process of accountability, more than anything else I've ever seen in sales, induces a salesperson to consistently succeed.

So in review, success through backward thinking calls for us to have our goals in writing; a written plan with specific activities; a system of measuring how many of those activities get done; and a system of accountability, so that one or more people keep tabs on how we are doing.

When I introduce this in a company, the salespeople don't stand up and cheer. They feel short-leashed. They find these requirements oppressive, as if they are not being given room. The attitude I find is this: "You're all over me. Don't you trust me?"

But once again, consider Nick Saban and John Wooden and other great coaches. They micromanage. They have systems and processes. Saban's players don't necessarily like all of the things he's putting them through, but the University of Alabama's record speaks for itself. And John Wooden, decades ago, did the same thing in basketball at the college level at UCLA. What I'm suggesting here is we can do the same thing in our businesses with systems and processes, and one of those is this concept of backward thinking. When you begin with the end in mind, you truly will be going places.

Visit www.leveragesalesmgmt.com for more on these winning sales processes.

CHAPTER 11

HALF OF SALES IS A HEAD CASE

"An empowered associate does not need to be motivated,
managed, or leveraged with top-down power."
— Kraig Kramers

Half of sales success has nothing to do with product, price, service, strategies, or tactics. Rather, it has to do with getting up in the morning and saying, "I'm going out and kicking some serious butt today." It's crucial, then, for salespeople to have the right attitude. I call it the five foundational laws for self-renewal.

THE LAW OF SELF-DISCIPLINE

The first law is the law of self-discipline: "Success comes from knowing what we should be doing, and when we should be doing it, whether we want to or not." says Jim Pratt

For a salesperson, that comes down to time management. My general observation of salespeople is they are not good at managing their time. They tend to be more reactive than proactive. But with self-discipline, they can improve that.

I ask my audiences what they think is the most productive day of the year. I get a variety of answers, but the true answer is the day before vacation. It is the most productive day of the year because workers have a list to get done; they're checking things off. If they can get all that done before they leave, they know they will feel more relaxed with everything buttoned up.

Consider how much more business you could generate if you worked every day as if it were the day before vacation. What if you had that list of key activities and you knocked it out on an everyday basis? How much more in sales might you write? Would you have done even 5 percent more in sales last year? Or would it be more like 30 percent? That's a huge improvement, just from being disciplined and focused on activities.

Another important concept of self-discipline and time management is this: If you don't have an assistant, you are an assistant. Let's say that you, as a salesperson, make $100 an hour. There are activities that should be done in the selling arena but not necessarily by the salesperson. As an example, we could hire somebody at $10 an hour to update our database and our contact management system. Salespeople generally don't like to sit in front of a computer, so it makes sense to pay someone a lot less to do the data entry for them.

I would say that would be a great investment for salespeople to make, because for every hour that they paid somebody $10 an hour, they would be a net $90 ahead. And so if you don't have an assistant, you are an assistant. You're not leveraging the growth of your business, and as a result, you're violating the law of self-discipline.

Salespeople should know how much they make an hour. Many salespeople work for commission only, or they have a portion of their income at risk with some type of a commission structure. Whenever I say they ought to be measuring how much they're making hourly, they reply that they don't get paid by the hour. Nonetheless, you can calculate how much you make an hour. Keep track of how many hours you work in a month. Then take the money you made that month, divide it by the hours, and that, in effect, is your hourly rate.

So if I make $100 an hour and after five minutes with a prospect I can see it's going nowhere, I would be better served to cut that conversation short and be on my way. But many salespeople, having finally found somebody who wants to talk to them, will log half an hour even with a poor prospect. That half hour cost $50.

And so my advice to salespeople is this: Time is money, and you should understand how you're spending your money. In other words, take care of how you spend your time. Once again, it's about leverage.

I joke with my audiences that if they have kids, they have in-house assistants right there. Just tell the kids that you're going to teach them a new videogame called Updating Your Database and Contact Management System, and you'll pay them $10 an hour to play the game, and you just ended up scoring big. You have relieved yourself of those activities you don't want to do and that don't pay well. Now you're able to get in front of more prospects and more customers and generate more business.

At least three times a day, I ask myself this question: "Is what I'm doing right now the highest valued activity I could be working on?" We all get distracted by activities that don't have the highest payoff. Today we have technological tools such as phones with multiple alarms. Mine is set to remind me three times a day to be involved in high payoff activities.

THE LAW OF RESPONSIBILITY

The second law is the law of responsibility: You are responsible for the outcomes you experience. Zig Ziglar, the renowned motivational speaker who passed away just recently, would have said it this way: "If it's meant to be, it's up to me."

The largest sales force I had was 2,600 salespeople. I took that company over in a turnaround situation. We ranked the people from the top—from the best performer to the bottom performer. There were 650 salespeople in each quartile.

The top quartile was generating 67 percent of the sales for the organization. The bottom quartile was producing less than 3 percent of the sales. As a sales manager, I understand that one of the things that I should do is really take a hard look at that bottom quartile, and the likelihood is that the people there are in the wrong spot. But before I sent them on their way, I grabbed 20 of them and put them in a conference room and said, in effect, "What's up here? What are you doing at the bottom?"

For the next two hours, all I heard were things unrelated to sales. These people talked about the poor economy; they talked about not having enough products; they talked about the price being too high; they talked about lousy customer service. Not one turned to me and said, "Well, we're at the bottom because we're just not very good at this job called sales."

But with the same product, the same price, the same service, the same economy, the same numbers, 650 other people did 67 percent of the sales because those 650 at the top understood this law of responsibility. And they said, every day, "I don't care about the product; I don't care about the price; I don't care about the economy. When I go out there today, I'm going to get more than my share."

THE LAW OF ATTRACTION

The third law is the law of attraction. If you really believe you can do something, or have something, or be somebody, you will create the circumstances and find the people to allow you to do, have and be.

Whenever I've met somebody who is enjoying success, I tend to find that person believes in the law of attraction. They tell me something like this: "Gosh, it's amazing how people just show up in my life who help to make certain things happen."

Over 50 years ago, Walt Disney came up with the idea of building the happiest place on earth in Anaheim, California. It was going to have Tomorrow Land and Adventure Land and Fantasy Land and all of what we know as Disneyland. He took his extensive business plan to a friend who owned and ran a bank. "I intend to build the happiest place on earth," he said, "and I need financing."

His friend read the business plan. "Walt," he told him, "you don't need a banker. You need a doctor, because this is a sick idea." Instead, Disney went to another bank to pitch the deal. And then to another. He got his funding on his three hundred and eighth sales call.

And so I challenge myself and my sales students with this question: When do you quit? When do you figure no one will be interested? If Disney had quit, we wouldn't have Disneyland. Fred Smith built Federal Express on the basis of a term paper for which he got a C-minus. If you really believe you can be, have, or do something, you will create the circumstances and find the people who will facilitate it.

That underscores the fundamental lesson here: Much of sales success has nothing to do with product, price, service, strategies, or tactics. Half of success at selling is in your head.

THE LAW OF EXPECTATIONS

The fourth law is the law of expectations. What happens in our lives is directly related to what we expect will happen. Another way of putting that is we are what we think we are.

I once was hired by a client in Southern California who had a mortgage company. I had been in the mortgage industry before, so I was a natural choice. This company made it easy on its salespeople; it had a terrific marketing program that made the phone ring regularly. They were using TV ads and newspaper and magazines and the Internet and direct mail, a wide variety of marketing methods to get customers to call about a mortgage.

The guy who hired me said, "I'm not getting as good a conversion rate as I need. My salespeople are not making enough loans out of the calls, and if you could get them to be better, that would be terrific."

On my first day, I spent about three hours listening to calls. No one knew I was in the building. Later I went to the owner/operator and asked, "So what's the average number of loans on a monthly basis done by an average guy out on the floor?"

"Eddie is the best we have in the building, and he does 17 loans a month," he said.

"Well, great for Eddie, but I didn't ask you that. I asked you what the average guy does."

"Like I said, Eddie's the king of loans here. He does 17 a month."

Now when the owner/operator doesn't answer your question twice in a row, what is he telling you? He's not telling you that he doesn't know the answer, but instead that he's embarrassed by the answer.

"Listen," I said, "if you don't give me the real number now, I'm going to leave and never come back. So what is the average number done on a monthly basis by one sales guy on that floor?"

"Three," he said.

"Three? You've got to be kidding me!" I said. "I just spent three hours listening in on the phone. If I were a sales guy with that quantity and quality of leads, I would do 100 loans in a month."

"You're crazy!" he said. "Eddie's the king of loans and he only does 17," to which I replied that I would slay the king. If I could do so many, the owner/operator said, maybe he should just hire me to do loans, not be a consultant.

"Why would you pay me to fish," I replied, "when I could teach all the guys on the floor to fish?" I explained to him the concept of leverage. "I tell you what," I offered. "Give me any guy on the floor other than Eddie, and in two months I'll have him doing more than 40 loans in a month."

"There isn't a guy out there who could do that," he said.

"Well," I said, "if that's what you believe and that's how you lead, then you might be right. I'm going to try a different way. So give me a guy."

He gave me a subpar performer—no surprise. I agreed to take on the challenge. The owner/operator couldn't stop laughing.

"You know what? This isn't just business now; this is personal," I said. "Let's make a bet on the side, on top of the fee for my service. If your pick doesn't do at least 40 loans in the month after next, I'll pay you $1,000. But if he does, you pay me $1,000, okay?"

The owner/operator agreed. So I go out on the sales floor and had a talk with "my student."

"Listen," I said, "if you did 40 loans or more in a month, how much money would that make you?" He said, "Jack, that's so much money, I would do anything for that." I said, "You just gave me the perfect answer. You're going to do what I say, when I say, how I say, and I don't want any back talk. Are you and I on the same page?" He said "Absolutely."

That kid worked hard. I couldn't have been prouder of him. But two months later, I had to pay $1,000 to the owner/operator. The kid had done 37 loans.

The following month, however, an interesting thing happened. Five guys on the sales floor did more than 40 loans in a month. I had changed expectations. Prior to that, the salespeople had thought that Eddie was a freak at 17 a month. But when they saw that the "student" could do 37, they got a glimpse of their own true potential.

And so my message to salespeople is this: Raise the bar. It's amazing how much more you're capable of doing in business if you just raise the bar. The law of expectations will govern your results.

THE LAW OF BELIEF

The last law is the law of belief. A belief is a guiding factor, principle, passion, or faith that provides direction in life. What is your stake in the ground? Where, as a salesperson, do you go when your business starts to tail off?

My own belief system as a salesperson is grounded in that concept of backward thinking that I detailed earlier. That had been fundamental to my beliefs since I was 13 years old, when I spent that summer interviewing successful people at the golf course and put in writing a game plan of where I wanted to be in four areas of my life by age 30, financially, professionally, educationally, personally. I knew that if I could write that plan down and be held accountable, I would succeed. That was 50 years ago and counting.

That's my own law of belief. That's my guiding principle. I know that if I am true to it, I will do extremely well and accomplish more.

And when performance falls off, all I need to do is go to my system of measurement and I bet the reason will be obvious.

. . . .

CHAPTER 12

MANAGING THE PIPELINE

"Salespeople who reach the highest levels of success
regularly weed out a lot of prospects."
— Jack Daly

E very salesperson should maintain three baskets, one called prospects, one called customers, and one called clients. You need to regularly take a look into those baskets and see who is where, and who is moving out of one basket and into the next.

We call this pipeline management. You want to look for every

> Upgrade the people who are in that pipeline. Don't fall victim to hardening of those arteries.

opportunity to upgrade the people who are in that pipeline. Don't fall victim to hardening of those arteries.

Prospects, by definition, are those people whom you would

like to be doing business with but currently are not. But once they buy from you once or occasionally, they move from the prospect basket into the second basket, which contains your customers. That's a good category, but there is a better one, and that's the client basket. Clients are people who do a lot of business with you regularly.

Let's say a salesperson represents a line of 10 products. A customer might buy one of those 10 products every three months. A client might buy 7 of the 10 on a monthly basis. A salesperson who has built a clientele doesn't worry about cash flow. He doesn't worry about making his house payment, or car payments, or other bills. And when he doesn't have to worry about those things, he can sell in the interest of the customer first.

Someone who is my client probably would buy from me even if he didn't need the product. I could sell to that person just because I needed the cash flow, but that wouldn't serve my best interest in building a career in sales. Over time, trust would erode. Instead, with a loyal clientele, I can nurture trusting relationships by consistently keeping their interests first.

> *The key is to call on the right people.*

Once again, you can see that the better salespeople end up writing more business as they call on fewer people. The key is to call on the right people.

CINDY'S SECRET

Years ago I worked with a salesperson named Cindy in our residential mortgage company. Cindy was the fortieth top producer in the industry nationwide. In a single year, her loan production was $186 million worth of business. There were entire companies in that industry that weren't generating $186 million dollars in loans in a year, and this was one person.

I have long studied top producers and tried to figure out how they generate so much business. There are common traits from industry to industry among the top producers. I found that 90 percent of Cindy's business came from just 12 clients. Too many salespeople call on too many people who don't deserve their attention.

Let's say that you were a salesperson calling on 50 people and I told you that you weren't getting enough business out of your territory and you'd better get busy. If you are like most people, you would go back in your territory and call on a lot more people. And that would be the wrong move on your part. Instead, you should identify the high-opportunity accounts and call on them more frequently.

As we have seen, selling is the transfer of trust, and people do business with people they trust. They get to trust the people they get to know, and they get to know the people they see more frequently. If you call on too many people in the marketplace, no one comes to trust you, and therefore they don't tend to do business with you.

INSPECT THE BASKETS

So the key for successful salespeople at this top quartile is to focus. You need to focus to succeed, and there is a system and process that helps salespeople to focus better. We call it "inspect the baskets." Every salesperson should do it once a month, but top performers do it weekly, and here is how they do it.

They examine those baskets and ask themselves: "Who's the number-one prospect I'm working on right now, so that if I landed that account, life would get really good? Who's number two? Who's number three? Who's number four?" And they work right on down the list.

For each propsect, the salesperson then asks, "When did I last contact, or 'touch,' that person? How often have I touched him or her in the last 90 days, and in what ways? What's standing in the way of that prospect doing business with us?"

After that, the salesperson turns his attention to his basket of customers: "Who's the number-one customer? How often am I touching that customer and in what ways? What's standing in the way of that customer becoming a client of ours?"

And then onward to the client basket. "Who's number one, two, and three?" The salesperson goes down the list. "How often is that client contacted, in what ways, and what stands in the way of doing more business with us?"

Any organization whose salespeople are not inspecting those baskets at least monthly is leaving business all over the street. So many of us have heard this expression before, but it's worth repeating: inspect what you expect. Better yet is to have the sales manager inspect the baskets. Once again, when this system is introduced, the salespeople don't cheer. Once again, they feel "micromanaged." But this system and process, done consistently, will be certain to give you increased sales and profits.

In this proactive management system, there is one more pipeline, and this one flows not from prospect to client but from client to prospect. And that pipeline is filled with referrals, because one of the best places to get referrals is from your satisfied clients.

CHAPTER 13

· ·

PERCEPTION OF VALUE

"In the factory we make cosmetics, but in my store we sell hope."
– Charles Revlon

Irst-time sales are not based on real value. They're based on perceived value. Customers who are engaging for the first time with a company for a product or service can't buy real value without ever having experienced what they will be getting.

For example, I do sales training. I can tell you success stories, and how my training works, and everything that is involved. I can give you my background and fill you in on what the experience will be like. But until you actually see the results for yourself, you haven't bought real value. You have bought perceived value. If you engage me a second time, or a third or fourth time, then you are basing your experience on real value.

What perception of value are you creating in your marketplace so people will go out of their way and/or pay a premium to do business with you? Again, the key word is "perception." Yes, you should spend time creating real value. That's absolutely essential. However, where businesses and salespeople miss out is they spend little to no time on creating perceived value. If you create perceived value, then you will find it easier to win over new customers and sell.

It's not only companies that have perceived value. Individual salespeople have it. Have you ever seen a customer decide to just come back later if a particular salesperson isn't there at the moment? That behavior is based on the perception of value that the salesperson brings to the party. Nobody else will do.

WHAT IS YOUR TIFFANY'S BOX?

Think of that little blue box or that little blue bag from Tiffany's. People assume any gift from Tiffany's will be great because of their perception of value. Tiffany is in the retail selling business and is known as a destination store. People buy there not because they happen to be walking past a store in a mall. Instead, they typically leave their home saying, "I'm going to go to Tiffany's today"—and there aren't many of them around.

On their drive to Tiffany's, they pass other jewelers, more convenient. Those won't do. They're going to Tiffany's. And they don't expect to cut a deal. They figure, "I'm going to Tiffany's today, and yes indeed it's going to be expensive." Would you like your customers to regard you that way?

I put this challenge to every one of my clients. What is your Tiffany's box? What is your Tiffany's bag? What is it about your company and about you as a salesperson that would cause people to go out of their way and pay a premium to do business with you?

I tell you this: If you can create that kind of perceived value, and that momentum, the selling will be far easier. You will have a strategic advantage.

THE STARBUCKS STAR

Starbucks is another example of perceived value. You may never have been to the company's first store at Pike's Place Market in the Seattle waterfront area. It is inauspicious, humble, and cramped, and there's nothing that appealing or special about the place. But look at what grew from there.

Perhaps I'm not the best person to be analyzing Starbucks because I've never had a cup of coffee—and people who know me say I shouldn't, since I have way too much energy without it—but my wife, Bonnie, loves the stuff. We live about a mile from a Starbucks, and she often asks to stop there when we drive past. In that same strip center, two other places sell coffee. She could go to one of those and be served quickly, but she always elects to go to Starbucks. There's always a line there, and from my perspective it doesn't move all that fast.

When I stand in line with my wife waiting for her to order this cup of coffee, I don't understand the language that people are speaking. It's a Starbucks language. Before there was Starbucks, it was easy to order a cup of coffee. It came with milk and sugar, or it didn't. Now, you can't buy a large cup. It's called a "venti," and they make it to your taste. They'll even put your name on the side of the cup. You buy it from a "barista," not a clerk.

Why are people willing to stand in line, particularly if it's their first experience with Starbucks? I've concluded that it's because other people do. They figure, "Gosh, this must be good."

That's the perception: "This must be good, in fact, so good that I'm willing to be inconvenienced." Tiffany & Co. is inconvenient. You have to go a long distance to get there. Starbucks is inconvenient, with that long line, and the cost is much higher than that of the competitors. And yet the Starbucks "experience" has grown into many thousands of stores worldwide. People behave the same way wherever you go. That's how Starbucks has built a competitive advantage. It's a clear example of perceived value.

THE APPLE IN YOUR EYE

Consider the laptop. Apple fans would have none other and pay more for the honor. Or the smartphone: People stood in line to buy the first iPhone for $600 with two years of mandatory service at $60 a month. It was a product that consumers had never seen, touched, or used. That is perceived value.

Steve Jobs and Steve Wozniak started Apple in a garage. Wozniak was the real value guy. Jobs was all about the perception game. Walter Isaacson's tremendous biography of Jobs makes it clear that the man knew how to create perceived value. As a result, Apple can charge a premium and have people waiting in line when its products are released.

Most buyers even keep the box that the iPhone comes in. I know that because I've asked my audiences. Apple spends time on packaging and presenting and creating perceived value.

It's all orchestrated with the idea that when you create such demand, people will go out of their way and pay a premium to do business with you. It's a tremendous competitive advantage, both for a business and for individual salespeople.

A WINE FOR EVERY TASTE

The wine industry has done a great job in creating perceived value. I'm a wine guy, and I have 1,100 bottles in my wine cellar at my house today, where I hold wine tastings regularly. I could buy a cabernet sauvignon from Napa Valley, a 2007, for $20. I could also buy that wine for $40 and $60 and $80 and $100. In fact, I've done that, put the bottles in velvet bags, numbered them, and then asked my guests to taste and rate them.

I often have seen $20 and $30 bottles of wine beat $100 bottles. The difference is that time has been spent cultivating the perceived value of the more expensive ones. A large portion of the price differential goes for company profit. If the $100 bottle of wine—or the Apple laptop—has a higher margin, then the companies can afford to pay their salespeople a higher commission.

When I ask my audiences, "Would you rather sell the $100 bottle of wine or the $20 bottle?" everybody chooses the former. And that's when I ask this: "Then why do I so often run into salespeople who complain that they would sell more if the company would just give them a lower price?" Create enough perceived value and the price won't matter.

OVERCOMING THE PRICE OBJECTION

The reason we get price objections is that we either haven't created enough perceived value or enough trust, or both. If you create enough of each, the price objection tends to diminish, if not entirely disappear. When a prospect does ask about price, he or she is thinking about buying, so be prepared to explain the benefits that person will value.

You can buy a watch that tells the correct time for $50, but you could also spend $10,000 on a watch. Now, there's a much greater margin in that $10,000 watch. When I ask my audiences, "Tell me the name of a company when I say 'watch industry,'" Rolex is usually one of the first mentioned. In the last several years of a tough economy, not one Rolex retail store has closed.

> When a prospect does ask about price, he or she is thinking about buying, so be prepared to explain the benefits that person will value.

Still, in a tight economy, many salespeople think that a lower price would be their only weapon to increase sales. The examples that I have given are companies that have done extremely well over the last five years. In the malls during the holidays, I saw stores boarded up because of the economy.

Meanwhile, at Tiffany's, people waited patiently in line for a chance to talk to a salesperson. They do that at Victoria's Secret too and pay a premium for lingerie that they could get cheaper elsewhere. Victoria does indeed have the secret. Harley-Davidson overcame its troubles by turning itself into a cult: People who have never been on a motorcycle will buy Harley-Davidson jackets, shirts, hats, even tattoos. If you order a bike, you wait weeks for its delivery, and if you are a fan, you do that gladly rather than go with the competition. General Motors has to sell seven cars to make in profit what Harley makes on one bike. It all illustrates the premium that people will pay for perceived value.

And keep in mind, individual salespeople have their perceived value. I don't reference their names here only because you do not know them but, their customers do and they buy accordingly.

LEVERAGING THE POWER OF THE INTERNET

A company can create perceived value by leveraging the power of the Internet. Before calling on a prospect, it's a good idea to visit that company's website. The purpose is to gather five or six questions or observations, such as these: Why does the company carry a product that its competitors do not, or vice versa? How is the company growing? What challenges are they having with a particular product or service? I'm looking for clues to questions such as those.

I also look for words or phrases that are repeated frequently. Those have been put in there intentionally by the web designers in the interest of something called SEO, or search engine optimization, which helps the company show up prominently in web searches. After I identify those words, I look at what comes up when I do my search. The results are companies or products in the same space that my prospect plays in. That means that those companies also could be my prospects. I will want to visit their websites and get several questions on each of them too.

I now have a dozen or so questions or observations, and when I sit down with the prospect, I can demonstrate that I have cared enough to do my homework. I can have a legitimate conversation about the business and whether my product or service can enhance what that company is trying to accomplish.

Now, that is so tremendously different from what typical salespeople are doing. The typical salesperson doesn't do the homework and essentially just knocks on doors, pulling stuff out to try to sell. People do not want to be sold. The salesperson's job is to help them to buy. The best way that you can help them to buy is help them with their needs, opportunities, and problems in the best way that you can. By coming to them armed with many questions and observations, you lay a foundation of trust. You create perceived value that diminishes or eliminates the price objection.

You demonstrate that you're not just schlepping products or services. You take your profession seriously and show that you want to help your prospects grow their businesses by educating yourself about them and their needs, goals, and their competition. Before the Internet, such research would have taken endless hours. Today it is at our fingertips 24/7, yet most salespeople miss this great opportunity.

As a salesperson, you personally can leverage the power of the Internet to build your career and make more money. Don't underestimate the reach of the social media as a way to leverage your perceived value. It's a good way to deepen relationships.

SHOW YOUR FACE ON FACEBOOK

A company recently came out with an initial public offering that put its valuation in the market at around $100 billion dollars. No company ever had an IPO with that high a valuation. Its name was Facebook. Even as stock prices fluctuate, the market is still saying that commerce is being done there in a significant way. And that means it's a place where a salesperson should be spending time. If you're in sales, you should be figuring out how to leverage your Facebook presence. Remember: people do business with people they like, so if friendships and relationships are built on Facebook, why would a salesperson not have a presence there?

People tell me they don't want to mix their personal and business lives. Why not? My mother said years ago, "You should run your life so that you wouldn't mind if anything that's going on in your life was on the front page of the paper." You shouldn't be embarrassed about what's going on in your life. In fact, the more you can share it, the more you will find in common with others.

I encourage people to friend me on Facebook, http://on.fb.me/1piz7Uz. I have today about 3,000 friends on Facebook. Now, if you were a friend on Facebook, you would find photographs of marathons I've run in my quest to do them in every state. Not everyone comments about them, but many of the runners whom I've friended will do so. We're building some relationship there. We're going deeper. Or golf friends will comment on photos I post in my quest to play a hundred top US courses. All that dialog is going on. If I post photos of my family and grandkids, one set of friends responds. If I do a wine tasting at my house, the wine lovers respond. If I do an Ironman, the triathletes respond. And so on.

Consider this: If I'm doing a workshop in a particular area, I ask my Facebook friends to hit the share button if they know anybody in that area who might be interested. I provide a link describing the workshop and how to register. Today 20 percent of those who attend my workshops had never heard of me before, but they came by way of a referral from a Facebook friend who hit that share button.

A woman recently came up to me at a workshop, gave me a big hug, and told me she knew I didn't know her but she'd been a longtime Facebook friend and that seven other friends of her's had come to the workshop because of her enthusiasm about meeting me personally. I charge hundreds of dollars a head for a seat at one of my workshops. This is what Facebook is doing for me in just that small arena.

DON'T MISS OUT ON LINKEDIN

LinkedIn is another important site for salespeople, and many of those in my audiences are on the site but don't know how to leverage its value. If you were linked in with me, **http://www.linkedin.com/in/jackdaly**, you would have access to over 3,000 others who are linked in with me. If any of those people were in your prospect basket and you'd had difficulty getting a meeting with them, you could e-mail me and ask for an introduction. I could probably make that happen more easily than you could by just banging on the prospect's door.

You need to figure out who is in your centers of influence. Who are the people you could leverage on LinkedIn to open doors for your sales? A LinkedIn referral is going to be much more valued than a stranger who comes knocking. Be active in a couple of groups in your industry. When someone posts a question asking for ideas or perspectives, respond early and often. That raises your perceived value as someone who knows his stuff. You'll become the go-to guy.

And be sure to complete your LinkedIn profile. If you are only 70 percent done with it, that percentage is placed on your home page and you come across as someone who only does things part way. You don't want to advertise that you're sloppy, untidy, or don't have your act together. That percentage needs to be reviewed monthly because the criteria for a complete profile changes from time to time.

You should work hard to link in with more than 500 people. Five hundred is a key number because then your profile will say 500-plus. If you try to link in with me and I look at your profile and it says you're linked in with 17 people, I'll be scratching my head and wondering, "Why would I want to link in with this guy? No one knows him. He's not busy, and he doesn't bring any real value to the party." I won't perceive much value in you.

THE PLAXO TOUCH

Plaxo alerts are also valuable to you personally as a salesperson. Every day, I get 5 to 10 Plaxo alerts. The alerts simply tell me about people's upcoming birthdays. Plaxo monitors your social media contacts, and gives you a heads-up on whoever is in your world.

How can that be beneficial for a salesperson? Here's an example. I was in Sydney, Australia, a couple of years ago and got a Plaxo alert that a client of mine was having a birthday the next day. He is the chairman of the board and founder of a company in Birmingham, Alabama, and has relationships with about 350 dealerships. Many of those dealerships have sales forces big enough that they could hire me as a sales trainer all on their own. My client's company also has relationships with 40 manufacturing companies, each of which also has a sales force big enough to warrant hiring me. The client has hired me on eight occasions, and I spoke a couple of times at the client's annual dealer and manufacturer conferences. All 350 dealers and the 40 manufacturing companies were represented in an audience of 500 or 600 people.

However, when I received the Plaxo alert, I hadn't worked with the client for about two years. I sent the chairman an e-mail: "Hi, I understand that your birthday isn't until tomorrow, but I happen to be in Australia, so you're already that old here, buddy. I didn't want to wait an extra day before wishing you a happy birthday. Go out and make it a terrific day. Remember this, Jack Daly loves you. From Australia, Jack."

Within an hour, I got an e-mail back from him: "Hey, Jack, it blew me away that you remembered my birthday, and it's even more impressive that you would take time out of your busy schedule while down under to wish me good tidings. When you get back to the states, call me. It's been too long since we've had Jack Daly visit us." Two weeks later, he scheduled me as keynote speaker at a conference with the dealers and manufacturers and invited me to golf with the top producers the next day. When I boarded the plane to go home, I had booked seven more speaking opportunities.

All of it started with a Plaxo alert. Most of the people in my audiences have no idea that Plaxo even exists. It's free. So is LinkedIn, and so is Facebook. What salespeople need to understand is that the Internet is a good tool for leveraging relationships, for touching customers, and to differentiate themselves from the competition.

OTHER INTERNET TOOLS

There are a variety of other Internet resources that salespeople can leverage. YouTube can be effective in increasing perceived value. I post one-minute and two-minute videos to YouTube all the time. Numerous people subscribe to my YouTube videos, http://www.youtube.com/user/mrjackdaly and I'm giving them moneymaking ideas regularly that way.

Salespeople should consider writing a blog. My recommendation is to publish a blog at least twice a month. It is not as important that people read it as it is to do it regularly because the more frequently you blog, the more impressive you are to the search engine optimization crew, which then increases your perceived value.

....

Sign-up for my newsletter at www.jackdaly.net.

....

VisibleMe.com is another tool that can be leveraged, and the list goes on and on. The Internet and social media space will continue to gain importance in the business world. New sites are popping up daily. Pinterest is a great example of a relative newcomer bearing great sales fruit. Those who are jumping on as a way to improve sales are finding great results.

CHAPTER 14

JUST THE RIGHT TOUCH

"Unseen—unheard—unsold."
— Unknown

L et's say that you operate a residential mortgage lending company. Who is your customer? Ninety-nine percent of the time, when I ask that question, people reply that the customer is the homeowner or the home buyer. But when I press for more, I get other responses: the builders, investors, banks, realtors, financial planners, insurance companies, title companies, appraisers. In any industry, the list is extensive yet unexplored in this way. The key is to ask "Who else?" many times over.

However, most people fail to think more broadly about who the customer might be, and they are missing opportunities to leverage those customers. You need to test yourself with a simple and persistent question: "Who else?"

In pursuing those customers, however, you need to create different perceived values for them. Each customer segment has different needs, and those needs should dictate how you create that value. If you think one size can fit all, you're going to blow it. Companies and their top salespeople are discovering that it makes great sense to identify how to segment their customers as they go about winning their business.

HOW MUCH IS THE CUSTOMER WORTH?

Using the same example, let's consider what the customer is worth. I'm going to assume a $100,000 mortgage loan. Years ago when I had that business, we made about $1,500 in profit in pretax income. Fifteen hundred dollars in profits was what a customer was worth, but we then learned to ask the next question: What is the lifetime value of a customer?

When we considered lifetime value, we had to figure out how many mortgage loans a typical customer would take out in his or her lifetime. What we found was seven: a first home, a relocation, a move-up, a second home, and three refinancings. It's easy to see how people get to seven in a lifetime.

Now, if you were to get all seven from that same customer, at $1,500 per loan, that would be worth nearly $11,000 to you. How many companies are getting all seven of those mortgage loans from the customer? The answer is not many, if any. Few get more than one.

The reason is that in so many situations, the salesperson gets the first sale and then goes knocking on the door of a new prospect. Instead, it's better to go wide and go deep with your existing customers. Get more out of that initial sale. The hardest sale you make is the first sale because you had to scale a hurdle called trust.

Once you've created the trust, then you go wide and deep with the accounts. What we mean by wide and deep is that if someone is buying a product from you regularly, and you sell 10 products, it's easier to introduce a few more of those products to that person rather than trying to get in other people's doors. If you're already doing business with two locations of a company that has 50 locations, it would be easier to win over a third, fourth, and fifth office in the chain with inside referrals than to find new customers. You have already laid down some trust.

If I hired you as a salesperson and said, "You can go after realtors or you can go after homebuyers but you can't go after both," which would you choose? Most all say they would choose the realtor, who is always in the business and can send them the buyers. That is a leverage opportunity. However, at the start of the exercise, I generally have to prod the audience before anyone suggests the realtor. The high leverage accounts that can robustly grow your business are not necessarily the first ones that come to mind. I could build 10 strong relationships with real estate agents and they could send me a continuing amount of business. That's a lot easier than trying to find each Tom, Dick, and Harry in the home buying sector.

In the exercise, I then suggest that we be choosy about the realtors we go after, and that brings up the Pareto principle of the Italian philosopher Vilfredo Pareto. It's also known as the 80-20 rule. Most businesses see some manifestation of that. Twenty percent of the people generate 80 percent of the business. That's why I tell my salespeople to focus on the real estate agents who generate the most business.

Let's say that you are one of my targeted realtors and I've built a great relationship with you. We're Facebook friends; we golf together. You sell two homes every month, like clockwork. Because of our relationship, I write a loan on one of those two homes every month. In five years, that's 60 loans. As I pointed out, I could parlay each into an $11,000 value over a lifetime, and by doing so, the value of the relationship with that agent would be $660,000.

It makes the most sense, then, to focus my time and resources on agents like that. And consider this: Those figures are based on a $100,000 loan, but when I was in the mortgage business, my average loan size was $500,000. In that case, the value of the business that such a strong relationship over a five-year period could eventually bring me would be worth more than $3 million in profits.

That exercise highlights the great opportunities in leveraging growth. I repeat: The better salespeople call on fewer people and write more business. The key, again, is that they call on the right people. The top 10 percent of salespeople focus on the right segment. Who are the "realtors" in your business?

THE TOUCH SYSTEM

Every salesperson and sales organization ought to have a "touch system." There are four databases of people for whom you need to build a touch system. The databases are prospects, customers, clients, and "other," or anyone we need in life who doesn't fit in the first three buckets. A lot of salespeople overlook the "others," who are centers of influence. You will recall my earlier example of the swim coach who recommended me to a bicycle shop. It's all about relationships.

What are touches? A touch is any way that you reach out and let somebody know you exist. A touch can be a personal visit, a phone call, an e-mail, a voicemail, snail mail, a fax, a social media contact. It says, "Hey, I'm out here." You can't sell if no one knows you exist or ever hears from you. Unseen, unheard, unsold.

Statistics indicate that it takes nine touches before someone knows that you exist, yet most salespeople and organizations quit at five or fewer. As a result, they misspend time, money, and resources by not touching them enough. Another mistake that companies and salespeople make is to focus those touches exclusively on their products and services. That approach is ineffective because of the rule that people don't want to be sold.

Unseen, unheard, unsold.

A good approach is to touch people in a variety of ways. You can touch them, for example, with information about their industry. You could touch them in ways to help them be better at their business. You could touch them with general business ideas that you have gleaned from your reading and from seminars and workshops. You can fax the information, or scan it and e-mail it as an attachment, or drop it off at their place of business, or send it through the mail. And let it stand on its own: This isn't the time to include a plug such as, "Hey, by the way, we're selling a new product," or "Look here, we got a great price on this."

Don't overlook the personal touch, as well. If I were in your database, for example, how might you try to touch me, based on what you can learn about me in this book? You might note that I'm an Ironman triathlete, that I'm a runner, that I like to fish and golf and drink wine. My wife is named Bonnie; we've been married for 44 years; and we have two grandchildren, Malcolm and Wyatt. But would similar information that you learn about your prospects, customers, and clients end up in your database? Most businesspeople concede to me that they don't keep records of such information, but it's some of the best stuff you could leverage.

Think of the value. For example, let's say I learn that a prospect enjoys golf. I have a golf book called *The Elements of Scoring* by

Raymond Floyd. I could get copies of that book for contacts who like to golf and write a note inside, such as this: "Hey, Tom, I know you're a golfer and this is a great book, but don't give it to your friends until you've taken all their money on the golf course! Have fun out there. Jack." I could do that within minutes for anybody in my database.

If a salesperson puts such personal information in the database, the value to the company continues even after that guy leaves. When a new salesperson fills that seat, he has at his fingertips all that personal intelligence that was gathered over the years, just waiting to be leveraged again and again.

Suppose the new guy finds out his predecessor didn't like to golf but comes across a contact who does. Here's how he might use that bit of information for a touch: "Hey, Harry was a good guy, but it was weird that he never liked to golf. I love golf. Why don't we find a good time to go out and knock the ball around?"

In my company, a brand-new sales guy with lists of prospects, customers, and clients who are new to him can make such touches. It's possible because we have a system and a process whereby every salesperson is expected to update all the personal information he or she learns about prospects, customers, clients, and "other." It's a highly valuable way to make you stand out from the competition.

WHO MOST DESERVES A TOUCH?

Once you have figured out who to touch and how to touch them, then you need to prioritize. You simply don't have the time to touch everyone equally, nor does everyone merit that attention. How do you go about prioritizing? You need to break down your prospects, customers, and clients into categories.

Think of these, for now, as A, B, C, and D. The A category are those who deserve to be touched every day with something in some way. Those in the B category might get touched once a week; C, once a month; D, once a quarter. As a salesperson, you could set that up in a contact management system. You know, or can figure out, who among your contacts is most worthy of touching and how often it would make sense to do so.

The touch system is another vehicle to increase your perceived value and to help you differentiate yourself from the competition. Again, not only do companies have perceived value but individuals also do, and there is no reason to wait until your company sets up a touch system for you. It's something you can develop for yourself, and you can do it now.

CONCLUSION

··

IRONMAN LESSONS LEARNED

W hen I took on the Ironman sport about six years ago, I didn't know how to swim and I hadn't been on a bike since I was a teenager. Now, I've competed in the Ironman World Championship in Kailua-Kona, Hawaii; the Half Ironman World Championships; and I represented Team USA in the Long Course World Championship Triathlon.

I find a lot of the same themes in both of these sports that I love— that is, the Ironman sport, and the sport of sales and sales management. Growing oneself and growing one's business have much in common, as I have learned in my journey.

Attitude is central to success, for example. Fifty percent or more of success at anything in life is a head case. It has to do with getting up in the morning and saying, "Give it everything that you've got." If you bring that to your business, or if you bring that to the Ironman sport, you have the differentiated advantage.

There are many days in the Ironman world when I don't want to get up in the morning and do that 5 a.m. run, and it's not easy to sit on a stationary bike for three hours watching some television show that I'd rather not see just because I need the training to prepare for that great day.

It's the same in sales. Some days, salespeople just have to make themselves get out in the field and make those face-to-face calls. You have to pick up that phone and take that share of rejection that you know will be coming. I say this: If you go about that business with a negative attitude, then your performance is going to be lacking. Whether it is race day or sales day, a positive attitude improves your game. Fifty percent is in your head.

You need a goal. Long before I knew how to swim, I set a goal to be in Hawaii competing in the Ironman World Championship. That goal dates back to some 30 years ago, when I watched Julie Moss crawl across the finish line in an Ironman competition.

I waited a long time before moving to fulfill that goal because I didn't have the time to train adequately when I had the responsibilities of children at home and employees in my company. But I put together a game plan. I built the systems of measurement and accountability and had people holding me accountable to achieving the goal of being an Ironman.

When I think about my businesses, whether I was owner, sales manager, or salesperson, I have taken the same path to success. The goals were in writing, the vision was clear. We had game plans for our salespeople and managers, and for the organization as a whole. We had systems of measurement to make sure we were doing what we needed to do, and we held ourselves and others accountable.

I have learned the importance of modeling the masters. You will find people who have already figured out how to do what you want to accomplish, and they know it better than you do. Year after year, I see the same salespeople at the pinnacle of success. They have the same product as the others, the same price, the same service, and yet they excel where others do not. I say they must be doing some things better. It's better to learn from others how to avoid mistakes than to learn from your own mistakes.

Wouldn't it make sense to let people like that coach you? Coaching is critical to success. In the Ironman sport, one must know how to swim properly. Once I couldn't make 25 meters in a pool, and now I find myself swimming 2.4 miles in deep water ocean, and I am achieving it at an incredible time. I can do that because I sought out a coach who taught me the effective and efficient way to swim and cut through the water, and still maintain an energy level that would enable me to do the bike and the run portions of the triathlon. Seek out those who know what they're doing, and learn from them.

> It's better to learn from others how to avoid mistakes than to learn from your own mistakes.

It takes training and practice. Nobody starts and finishes the Ironman without an abundance of both. In fact, nobody excels at any sport without training and practice. And that's true too in the sales arena and in the business world. If you want your business to run well, if you want your sales to grow at a more robust pace than those of your competitors, you need to practice and train, train, train. If you are not training, you are not gaining.

Your support team will help you. You need one. My wife has been to every one of my Ironman races. On race day, the wakeup call is at 4 a.m., and there's Bonnie, helping me with my breakfast and then taking the equipment down to the race site for the 7 a.m. start. Then after that is a long 112-mile bike race, and then a 26.2-mile run, and there is my loyal, devoted cheering section, my support team, my Bonnie. And along the way, regardless of the weather, are many others out there all day giving me encouragement. I need my bike coach, my running coach, my nutrition coach, my strength coach. These are my support team.

Salespeople too need a support team. If they try to do all things themselves, they are not exercising the concept of leverage. If they don't have an assistant, they are an assistant. You need support from operations and from marketing, and you need to manage your contacts. It all comes together in the business world just as it does in the triathlon sport. Success in any endeavor requires a support team.

And whatever the endeavor, you need to stay fit if you want to stay in the game. I have known the rigors not only of the Ironman sport but also of the business world. Some days the hurdles are high and you have to hustle to put out fires. If you eat right and exercise, you can rally the energy to get to the top and stay there. The sales world itself is full of rejection, massive amounts of it. You need the stamina to get beyond that to victory.

YOU CAN DO IT

I mentioned that, nearly three decades ago, I watched Julie Moss, who is legendary in the history of the Ironman, crawl across the finish line in Hawaii after a feat of swimming, bicycling, and running. What we human beings are capable of is astounding to me.

I decided at the age of 57 to move forward with the Ironman challenge. The swim portion of an Ironman competition is 2.4 miles. Though I couldn't swim, I believed I could do it. All I needed to do, I told myself, was hire a coach, learn the technique, and devote myself to practice.

And here I am, just a few years later, with a successful finish in the World Championship Ironman. It has come about through discipline. We bring into our lives the very things that our attitude attracts.

As we pursue greater heights, the opportunities come to us from all directions. I feel it's my duty to raise the bar.

It's your duty too to raise the bar. You must risk believing in yourself. Until you test the limits regarding what you can achieve, you can't truly know what your chances really are. The major obstacle to overcoming the odds is never challenging them.

> Until you test the limits regarding what you can achieve, you can't truly know what your chances really are. The major obstacle to overcoming the odds is never challenging them.

As the leader of a company, you can develop a winning culture that will have people knocking at your door for a chance to work with you. As a salesperson, you can learn the tricks of the trade that will drive you to ever-greater heights. For the company and for the individual, your business is poised to soar.

SALES SUCCESS SUMMARY

On sales:

- Never make a call without a purpose.
- Ask questions and listen.
- Never quote price until you establish value.
- Trust trumps price all day long.
- The best salespeople are canned. Don't wing it.
- Model the masters. Learn from the best.
- People are different. Sell accordingly.
- We are what we think we are. Raise the bar!
- If you don't have an assistant, you are an assistant.
- Practice leverage.

TIPS FOR COMPANY LEADERS

- Successful cultures need to be intentionally managed.
- Implement minimum standards of performance. Negotiate individually.
- Hire slowly; fire quickly. You are never "fully staffed."
- Recruiting is a process, not an event. Put your prospects in writing and court them.
- Recruit for skills; hire for attitude. Fifty percent of success is attitude.
- Implement an orientation program for new hires. Start with a celebration.

- Coach on the field, not in the locker room. Training equals gaining.
- Focus performance looking ahead, not behind. Develop and conduct quarterly one-on-ones.
- What are your systems to ensure consistent and regular recognition?
- People are different. Lead accordingly.
- Model the masters. Align the new with the experienced.
- A sales leader's job is not to grow sales. It's to grow salespeople in quantity and quality.

APPENDIX III

TIPS FOR SALESPEOPLE

- First impressions count. Be unique, from reception to voicemail.
- Goals not in writing are dreams.
- Things that get measured get done. Develop key metrics, track regularly, and be accountable to others for your goals.
- The short course on selling: Ask questions and listen. Stop showing up and throwing up.
- Fifty percent or more of success is a head case. Have the right attitude.
- People buy on perception. Design and promote your perception of difference.
- Focus precedes success. Customers should not be treated equally.
- People are different. Sell accordingly.
- The best salespeople are canned. Don't wing it.

- Answer these questions uniquely: Why you? Why your company?
- Model the masters. Learn from the top performers.
- Professionalism requires lifelong learning. Instill a program of books, audio/videos, and seminars.
- Success is in the palm of your hand. Reach for it!

APPENDIX IV

CHECKLISTS

Focus Precedes Success

Sales Leadership Checklist
- Rank sales staff performance and deal with poor performers;
- One on ones with each sales professional, minimum monthly;
- Sales meetings twice monthly minimum;
- Recruiting basket of at least 15 we are courting;
- Recruiting courting process built around a touch system;
- Recruiting interviews ongoing;
- Inspect the baskets (pipeline management), minimum monthly;
- Inspect key activities of sales professionals;
- Progress reviews at least quarterly;
- Training, training, training to include role practice, joint calls, training calls, coaching calls and building a success guide;
- Inspect monthly the sales professionals touch system;
- Recognition activities, ongoing;

- Rewards systems, ongoing, including contests;
- Compensation plans—review twice yearly;
- Key account focus;
- New hire orientation;
- Unit performance management (actual/plan analysis);
- Senior management interactions (proactive/reactive).

Sales Systems and Processes Checklist

- Goal setting
- Key activities ID
- Key activities tracking and measurement
- Pipeline management
- Time management
- Leveraging the internet
- Objection ID and responses
- Question guide: what and when to say
- Differentiating from the competition processes
- Proactive database leveraging
- Recognition systems for prospects/customers/clients

Jack Daly is an expert in sales and sales management inspiring audiences to take action in customer loyalty and personal motivation. He delivers explosive keynote and general session presentations.

Jack brings 20 plus years of field proven experience from a starting base with the CPA firm Arthur Andersen to the CEO level of several national companies. Jack has participated at the senior executive level on six de novo businesses, two of which he has subsequently sold to the Wall Street firms of Solomon Brothers and First Boston. As the head of sales, Jack has led sales forces numbering in the thousands, operating out of hundreds of offices nationwide.

Amongst a career of highlights, here are a couple of noteworthy examples:

- In 1985, Jack relocated to California from the east coast and started a mortgage company with 3 colleagues. As CEO, Jack lead the company through robust growth in its initial 18 months to 750 employees, 22 offices nationwide, producing $350 million per month in mortgages, and it's first 3 years the company reported profits of $42 million.
- In 1998, working as a senior partner in a 5 year-old privately held Enterprise, Jack helped the company to be recognized as Entrepreneur of the Year by Ernst & Young and ranked #10 on the Inc. 500 list of the fastest growing firms nationwide.

Personal Highlights include:
- Jack has been married 43 years to his high school sweetheart.
- In 2007, Jack completed his first Ironman in the United Kingdom.

- Jack has now completed twelve Ironmans in eight countries, on five continents, and made team USA in 2012.
- Jack has played golf at over 80 of the Top 100 golf courses in the USA.
- To date Jack has completed 57 marathons over 30 states in the USA.
- Jack has bungee jumped the world's first and world's largest bungee jumps, and shark dived in South Africa.

Born and raised in Philadelphia, Jack currently resides in San Clemente, California.

WHYjackDALY? JACK SPEAKS FROM EXPERIENCE

1. History of proven growth of clients businesses from individual success stories to international size firms.
2. Proven CEO/Entrepreneur, having built 6 companies into national firms.
3. Co-owner/senior exec, of INC #10 and Entrepreneur of the Year award winner.
4. Vistage UK Overseas Speaker of the Year.
5. TEC Australia Speaker of the Year.
6. Spoken to audiences in several countries on 5 continents.
7. BS Accounting, MBA, Captain in U.S. Army, accomplished author of books, audio and DVD programs.
8. Led sales forces numbering in the thousands.
9. Competed in the Ironman World Championship. Is an Ironman on five continents.

RESULTS – that's what all of the above is about. Jack Daly delivers results.

FOR MORE INFORMATION ON JACK DALY SERVICES

Speaking: Call Jennifer Geiger 888-298-6868

 Jack delivers explosive keynotes, general session presentations, workshops, seminars and training sessions that inspire audiences to take action in the areas of sales, sales management, corporate culture, customer loyalty and personal motivation.

Workshops: Call Adam Daly 855-733-7378

 Jack's sales workshops, sales management programs, and performance seminars are ideal for owners, executives, and sales personnel looking to grow sales profitably and increase competitiveness.

Leverage Sales Coaching: Call Dan Larson 916-972-1292

 We help you get sales right. The right people, the right systems, and the right leadership help to grow results by Jack Daly design. We deliver a customized coaching plan focused on achieving your sales growth goals: assessment and strategy, skill development, action game plan, and accountability to action.

Training Tools: ww.jackdaly.net/content/dvd-and-cd-tools

 A digital library that features Jack Daly's business acumen is available for purchase. The comprehensive collection features lessons on corporate culture, sales management, sales skills, and growing a business among others. Each of these topics are available in either an audio CD or DVD format. Get motivated with Jack!

Online University: www. http://jackdalysalesu.com/

 The Jack Daly's Sales U curriculum was designed to provide Entrepreneurs & CEOs, sales managers, and sales professionals the tools, knowledge, and application to successfully sell in today's hyper-competitive business environment. Jack Daly pulls back the curtain and leaves no stone unturned. When you complete the curriculum, you will have the tools and knowledge to grow your sales and management teams in quantity and quality, and effectively build a culture that attracts A-players.

Newsletter Signup: http://www.jackdaly. net/content/newsletter-sign-up/

 Sign up to get valuable sales ideas that Jack Daly's clients use to grow their business and increase profitability. Start thinking, acting, and selling more effectively today!

How can you use this book?

MOTIVATE

EDUCATE

THANK

INSPIRE

PROMOTE

CONNECT

Why have a custom version of *Hyper Sales Growth*?

- Build personal bonds with customers, prospects, employees, donors, and key constituencies
- Develop a long-lasting reminder of your event, milestone, or celebration
- Provide a keepsake that inspires change in behavior and change in lives
- Deliver the ultimate "thank you" gift that remains on coffee tables and bookshelves
- Generate the "wow" factor

Books are thoughtful gifts that provide a genuine sentiment that other promotional items cannot express. They promote employee discussions and interaction, reinforce an event's meaning or location, and they make a lasting impression. Use your book to say "Thank You" and show people that you care.